Ahwahnee
An Indian Tale

Ahwahnee
An Indian Tale

by
Wandering Poet, M.A.

Gone Fishin' Press

copyright©2011 by wandering poet
all rights reserved
ISBN: 978-0-578-05433-9

Author's Note

Although this book is fiction, it is historical fiction. The information offered regarding Indian culture--i.e., hunting & gathering, shelters, food, clothing, tool making, fire making, etc.--is well researched and accurate. Some of the events in the fictional story are taken from history, though they may be altered and rewoven. The part of this story that speaks of the first discovery of Yosemite Valley by white men is historically accurate and agrees with the known facts, though it presents events from the Indian point of view, rather than from the white perspective.

Some of the photos used to illustrate this tale are by Edward S. Curtis. His photos offer a window on Native American culture that posterity would not enjoy without his vision and effort. The Edward S. Curtis collection is housed at Northwestern University.

The photo of the "Paiute Village in Ahwahnee" is by Eadweard Muybridge.

The photo of the "Milling Boulder" is by George Fiske.

The photo of "Ahwahnee Paiute Suzie McGowan & Daughter" is by J. T. Boysen, c. 1901.

The lithograph of "Paiute Women and Children in Ahwahnee" is by Boyle, c. 1891

All of these photos and the lithograph are in the public domain.

The photo of the "String of Mountain Brook Trout" is by Jasper Monti, San Francisco, a modern hunter/gatherer

The photo of "Rock Chief" (El Capitan) is by Steve Lundeberg, Albany, Oregon, Associate Editor, Democrat-Herald.

The photo of "The Sand Dunes" is by John Sullivan.

Paiute Women & Children in Ahwahnee
by Boyle, c. 1891

History

In 1849 gold was discovered at Sutter's Mill in the western foothills of California's Sierra Nevada Mountains. Until that time, many different tribes of Indians had lived in peace in these mountains, for thirteen thousand years. The populations were not large, and the environment provided enough to support them all. They lived as nature's guests, harvesting fish, game and plants for food, medicine, clothing, shelter and fire. They lived in harmony with nature, grateful for the living she provided, and they were not greedy for more. They were keenly aware of their place in nature and sensitive to the beauty of their mountain home. Each tribe had its own valley or canyon to live in, with hunting, fishing and gathering rights clearly defined. The high country, above the canyons and valleys, at elevations of 7,000 feet and higher, was shared territory. Anyone could gather food or hunt and fish there.

The various mountain tribes were gentle, peace loving people who lived largely without war or fighting. There was plenty of food and other resources for all. The only killing they did was to medicine men. If disease or hard times hit the tribe, they might kill the medicine man. Either he was intentionally causing problems, it was thought, or he was incompetent. Either way, he was finished as a medicine man. Otherwise the tribes lived in relative peace and harmony. There were petty quarrels. But killing was rare. In fact, even the corporal punishment of children or the beating of one's wife were shameful behaviors.

There was much trading between tribes and families. The Mono Lake Paiutes, for example, on the east side of the Sierra, had plenty of obsidian for arrow points and knives, salt, pinion pine nuts, and kuzavi, a desirable high-protein food product made of dried alkali fly larvae. But they did not have plenty of acorns or dried fruits and berries or trout or seashells or arrow shafts. These and other goods were traded for with the tribes in the foothills west of the Sierra, or in the canyons and valleys in the mountains.

When gold was discovered at Sutter's Mill, thousands of white men swarmed into the Sierra in search of the yellow metal. They were rough and greedy men, with a lust for gold. They tore up the land, wantonly depleted the game supply, killed Indians wherever they saw them, took Indian girls against their will for wives and servants, and cut down many oak and pine trees, for their buildings, fires and mining operations, trees which the Indians needed to harvest staple food crops of acorns and pine nuts. And there were some traders who set up trading posts in the foothills west of the mountains to supply the miners. These traders were also rough and greedy men, hungry for gold, many of whom took advantage of the miners, as well as the friendly Indians who chose to trade in their stores.

Indian tribes at first ignored the influx and tried to live with the white intruders. However, there were too many. The Indians could not ignore the damage they did to the land, the depletion of game reserves, the growing numbers of Indians that were being killed or kidnapped, the growing numbers of food trees that were being destroyed. These things threatened their very existence. Eventually these acts angered the Indian populations. The tribes organized, held councils and decided to kill the white miners and traders, throughout the entire 500 mile long mountain range, in an effort to drive the white men out of the mountains and keep their own homes, lives and food supplies secure.

By this time much of the California coast and central valley had been settled. San Francisco and Los Angeles were young though growing centers of commerce. The general population was a larger cross section of white society than just miners and traders. They had homes and families and businesses, and political influence. When word spread of the Indian killings of miners and traders in the mountains, the general population became alarmed and raised an outcry heard by the governor, who authorized and funded the formation of a civilian quasi-military group, consisting almost entirely of the miners and traders that the Indians had chased out of the mountains. This group was authorized to enter the mountains and kill or drive out all the Indians and herd them onto reservations that had been established in the central valley.

The last of the Indians to hold out were those in Yosemite Valley, at the time a remote and inaccessible place that the Indians believed the white men could never find or penetrate. The Valley was easy to defend, since the only entrance from the west was along the Merced River from Mariposa. When intruders tried to approach the Valley, the inhabitants would push rocks and boulders down on them from above, creating rockslides that discouraged further efforts at intrusion.

The Mariposa Battalion, a mounted and armed force of 200 determined miners and traders, finally entered Yosemite Valley in March, 1851, and again in May of that same year, to round up and drive out the Indians who lived there. These were the first white men to ever enter Yosemite Valley. They went there expressly to kill Indians or drive them from their mountain home. They killed those Indians who offered resistance, including Chief Tenaya's youngest son, and herded the rest of the tribe like cattle, out of their mountain home, to a reservation on the Fresno River. And that was the end of free Indian culture in the Sierra Nevada.

But this story begins in another place and time....

Chapter One

When Jesse and his sister, Sam, finished school for the year, the whole family packed up and headed out for their summer vacation. The family went on a vacation together every year. They had vacationed in places like Italy and Hawaii, at resorts in the Caribbean and Mexico, and in Yosemite National Park. But this summer they would do something they had never done before, something exciting, something Jesse had wanted to do ever since he could remember. They were going to take a 250 mile long raft trip down the Colorado River through the Grand Canyon!

The family consisted of Jesse, age 14, sister Sam, age 12, their mom and dad, and their dog, Moochi, a black and white Tibetan terrier. Sometimes Moochi got to go on vacation with them. But this year Moochi had to spend the vacation with aunt Nancy. He was a house dog. They did not think he would like the raft.

The family rented a 4-wheel drive wagon, loaded up their gear and headed for Page, Arizona. In Page, the family stayed in a motel the first night and had dinner in a Mexican owned Chinese-Pizza place, not far from the motel. The food was terrible. But no one cared. They were on vacation! After dinner, there was an orientation meeting with their river guides and fellow travelers. The next morning after an early breakfast, they drove down to Lee's Ferry, the launch site for the rafts, not far below the dam that backed the river up and made Lake Powell. All the rocks and the sand were red, and the canyon walls were red and orange and purple. The sky was turquoise blue, clean and clear. Jesse had lived in a city all his life, so he had never seen the sky so blue. He had never seen red sand or red rocks. The turquoise sky and red rock cliffs made a striking contrast. It was like being inside a painting or a picture postcard.

The family unloaded their gear, and the guides helped them stow their things in waterproof bags. Jesse and Sam and mom and dad helped the guides load the bags onto the raft. Everyone donned lifejackets, boarded the raft, and they were off! The raft drifted lazily along the gentle river. At first, the riverbanks were half a mile wide, and flat; the cliffs were low in the distance, the river wide and slow. As they moved along, the riverbanks narrowed and the cliffs drew closer and taller until the canyon walls came right to the water's edge. And soon the red cliffs towered a mile above their heads, the turquoise sky surmounting all. The scenery was breathtaking. And the view changed around every bend in the river.

The group drifted, at times on calm water, and at others the raft bucked up and down on faster, wilder water. Sometimes the ride was like a roller coaster, or a bucking horse, and the passengers became thoroughly soaked from the spray. The air was very warm, so the soakings were more welcome than not.

In the evenings, the guides chose wide sandy beaches where the group stopped, unloaded the boat and set up camp. There was a shared kitchen area, and each pair of travelers had their own tent. They made campfires to sit by, one of Jesse's favorite things to do. And he loved to see the stars. In a city you can't see very many stars. Until you are far away from the lights and pollution of a city, you cannot believe how many stars there really are in the sky. Some travelers preferred to sleep beneath the stars without a tent. Jesse liked to sleep out next to the campfire so he could look up and see the stars.

The time flowed swiftly by. Too swiftly. Very soon they had only two days left on the river. Then something strange happened that might never be explained. The group had traveled more than 200 miles. It seemed like they were spending more time in rapids than in calm water. During a particularly wild stretch, Jesse was thrown high in the air, and the raft shot out from under him. He landed in the water! He sped along on the current behind the raft, bumping into rocks, being pulled under water, then bobbing to the surface, gasping for air, being pulled under again.

He could see glimpses of the raft with the others on board, moving farther and farther ahead of him. The others could not see his small head bobbing in the churning water so far away. He called out but they could not hear him over the rushing sound of the water. Then he must have hit his head on a rock and lost consciousness. Because, the next thing he knew he was waking up on a sandy beach, and it was dark. There were stars overhead, silhouetting the rim of the deep canyon.

He sat up, startled, looking all around. There were no tents, no campfire, no raft, no people. He was completely alone in the dark night and soaking wet. Thankfully it was a warm night. He had nothing with him, only the few things in his pockets. His backpack was still on the raft. He had no food or water, no jacket or warm clothing, no way to make a fire. He sat on the sandy beach in the dark night, hugging his knees and shivering. The night was not cold.

Brush House Common to Western Desert Tribes

Chapter Two

Jesse sat in the sand, hungry and shivering, wishing he were with his family, wondering what he should do. Suddenly he had a sensation of being watched. He felt a presence, very close. The back of his neck tingled. He turned and looked to his side and saw two big eyes looking at him, and the dark shadowy shape of a large animal. Something was there, something big, crouching on the earth, close enough to reach out and touch! At first, Jesse thought it was a mountain lion. His heart stopped. But then the shadow spoke! "What a wretched sight!"

Silence. Jesse was startled. Here was a human being. But what kind of human being? He was not from the rafting party. Who was he? How did he get here, in the bottom of the Grand Canyon, so many miles from civilization? Was he friendly? Or dangerous? As these questions and others flooded Jesse's mind, the stranger spoke again. "Come."

The shadowy figure rose and walked away from Jesse and disappeared into the dark. With no other choice, Jesse jumped up and followed. They walked perhaps a mile along the beach. Then Jesse noticed not far ahead the flicker of a campfire. His heart leaped! Could this be his family and the rafting party?

As they drew close, Jesse could make out a cluster of huts made of sticks and grass. Most of them had three walls and an open front. Several of them had a small fire in front, to reflect heat into the interior, with a small pile of dry brushwood by the fire. People were sitting on the ground, inside and outside of the huts. But these were not the rafting party. They were not any kind of people Jesse had ever seen before. Their skin was very dark and leathery, from exposure to the sun and wind.

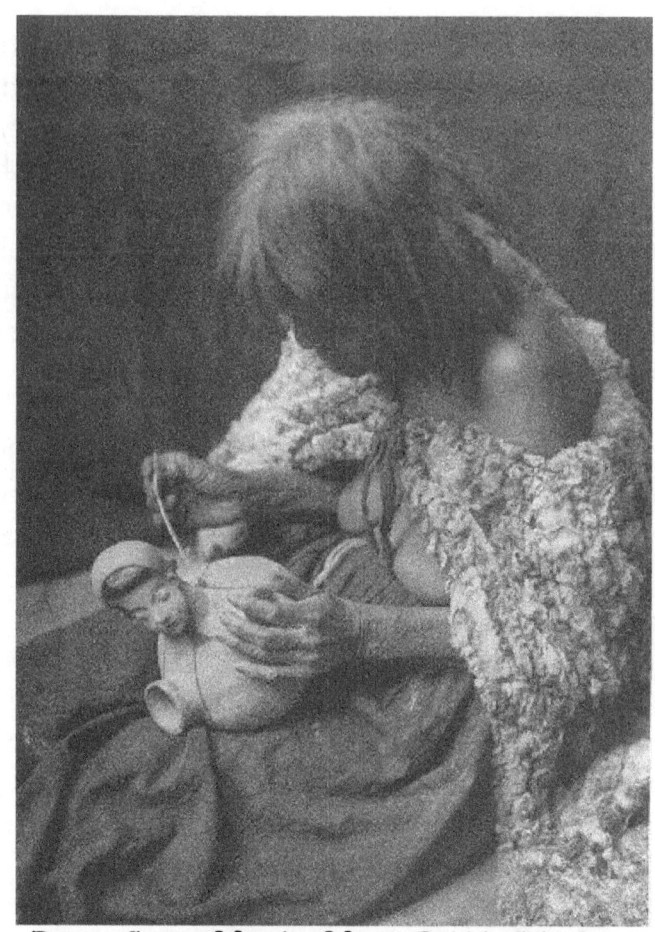
Desert Squaw Wearing Woven Rabbit Skin Cape

The men and women were all naked, except for leather loincloths, or short skirts split down both sides. Some of the women wore woven rabbit skin capes tied around their naked shoulders. The men wore their hair in two braids; the women wore their hair long and unbound, or gathered and tied back in a pony tail. One woman sat on the earth painting designs on a beautiful clay pot. The ground inside the huts was bare earth, swept smooth and clean. Naked children of various sizes were present, and a few dogs. Beds were piles of dry grass with soft animal skin covers and woven rabbit skin blankets. There were baskets of all sizes and shapes sitting on the ground, inside and outside the huts, and hanging on the walls of the huts. One woman used a muller on a flat stone metate to make some kind of flour. The aroma of roasting meat was in the air.

Jesse was astonished, and curious. Who were these people? They looked like Indians. But Jesse had never heard that there were any Indians living in the Grand Canyon. His young guide led him to one of the huts, where a brown and wrinkled old man in a leather loincloth sat on the earth tending a small fire.

Addressing himself to the old man, the boy said "I found this white boy all wet and sitting in the dark a mile down the shore." Then to Jesse, "This is Crow Dog, the village medicine man."

"Take off your wet clothing and sit by the fire," said the medicine man. "We will bring you some food." He motioned to the ground beside the fire. Jesse removed his life preserver, wet T-shirt and crash helmet. But he could not bring himself to take off his cargo shorts. As he sat cross-legged on the earth facing the fire, a woman handed him a small round basket containing something that looked like a brownish colored cereal, and a short, flat wooden spoon.

"When anyone comes to our village, it is our custom to offer food, drink, and shelter. Please, eat," said Crow Dog, making a motion of holding a bowl in one hand while scooping food to his mouth with the fingers of the other. Jesse was hungry for sure. He took a tentative taste. It tasted slightly sweet, with a licorice flavor, not bad. Jesse ate. After he finished the food, he sat observing, taking in everything. The Indians did not talk much. When they spoke it was in soft voices. They seemed gentle people, very relaxed and peaceful. Some of them tended the small fires and made food in front of their huts; one woman wove a basket; a mother nursed a baby; some people sat or lay on the beds inside the huts. Somewhere a woman sang softly, a plaintive, haunting refrain. It was a very peaceful and comforting atmosphere in the village.

Chapter Three

Jesse did not remember going to sleep. But when he woke the next morning he was lying in one of the huts on a sheepskin and grass bed. Someone had put a rabbit skin blanket over him. It was silky soft. He sat up suddenly and looked around. It was not a dream. The village was real. And he was really lost.

Some of the Indian women were tending fires and preparing food. The boy who found him was nowhere to be seen. Crow dog was not present. Jesse was alone in the hut. Soon a woman brought him a basket bowl of the same cereal he had eaten last night, and placed a flat wicker basket on the ground in front of him. On it were two small roasted legs of meat the size of chicken legs, and a piece of roasted green vegetable. The roasted meat smelled good. Jesse tore off a little piece and tasted. It was good! So was the vegetable. He ate everything.

As Jesse ate, the Indian boy approached and sat down. In the daylight Jesse could see that they were both about the same age. "I see you like rabbit meat," the boy said.

"Yes," replied Jesse, "I do. It's very good. What's this cereal?"

"Mesquite beans," replied the boy. "My name is Many Roads. "When you are finished with the food, I will take you to Crow Dog. He knows who you are and that you are lost. He has asked me if I will be your guide and lead you home. I have agreed."

"Thank you," Jesse replied.

"I hope your way does not take us through Apache country. Their lands stretch from here far to the east, and south into Mexican territory," said Many Roads. "I might travel through Apache lands by myself. But they would kill any white they find there, and they would probably kill me for bringing you there."

"Why would they kill me?" asked Jesse.

"Because you are white. The Apaches hate the Mexicans, and the whites. For many lifetimes, the Mexicans have raided the Apache villages, killed their people, taken their horses and food supplies, stolen their women and children, burned their homes. Now, the whites are doing the same things. So the Apaches kill any Mexicans or whites they find in their territory."

"My home is many miles west of here, in California," said Jesse. "Do you live here in this village?"

Many Roads replied, "No. These are Chemehuevi people. I am Paiute. My home is in the mountains far to the west."

"How did you get here," asked Jesse?

"I walked. That is how I got my name," said Many Roads. "I always like to see other places and people. I can go everywhere. I walked here, visiting different villages and tribes along my way, seeing how they hunt, what they eat, how they build their houses, seeing different kinds of territory. Very different are the deserts and the mountains and the marshlands and the plains. Sometimes, when our chief wants to send messages to other villages and tribes, he will send me. I have seen many roads."

The thought puzzled Jesse. Many Roads spoke as if there were Indian villages and tribes everywhere, and Apaches that kill people. He was finished with the meal. Many Roads rose and Jesse followed him. As they walked, Jesse heard the sound of laughter and voices. In the daylight, he could see that the village was by a stream that flowed into the river from a side canyon. He saw a group of women and children in the stream, bathing and playing together in the morning sun.

They arrived at another hut, where Crow Dog sat on the ground. As the boys approached, he motioned for them to sit. They took a seat opposite Crow Dog, who sat in silence for what seemed like a long time. Then he spoke to Jesse: "I have been expecting you. You are a long way from home. You are lost." This was a statement, not a question. Another long silence followed. How could Crow Dog have been expecting him?

Crow Dog spoke again: "You are lost, and you will not find your way without a guide. Many Roads will be your guide and lead you home." With that, Crow Dog rose and walked away.

"Here are your things. We can begin when you are ready," said Many Roads. Jesse saw his T-shirt, sandals, life jacket and crash helmet lying on the ground, and two rawhide water flasks with wooden plugs in their mouths, and a leather strap for hanging on the shoulder.

He surveyed Many Roads, who stood barefoot, in a soft leather loincloth, his hair in two black braids. Tied at his waist was a pair of moccasins, and a handmade flint knife, with a rawhide wrapped handle, in a stiff rawhide sheath. Over his shoulder was a red fox fur quiver full of arrows, and a spotted wildcat fur bag, about ten inches across. In his hand he held a wooden bow about four feet long.

"Where are we going?" asked Jesse.

"Home," said Many Roads.

"Now? We're going to walk? From here?" asked Jesse.

"Yes," said Many Roads. "The river runs west from here. But there are many steep rapids. Boats are no good. So we walk. We will leave the river and go southwest from here. There is a very old *Zuni road that goes from their pueblo east of Apache country; it runs west through Apache lands, to this river after it has turned south again. This river is the extreme northern and western limits of Apache territory. If we walk southwest from here, we will find the Zuni road and follow it west to the river. In this way, we will return to the river beyond the rapids.

*The ancient Zuni road referred to by Many Roads connected Zuni Pueblo, near Albuquerque, New Mexico, with other pueblos and villages across New Mexico and Arizona, then with the Colorado River and points west. The road may pre-date the Zunis, since it passes by several ancient Anasazi cliff dwellings and may have been created at least in part by the Anasazi, who were known to trade with Mexico and the west coast. When whites came and took the country from the Indians, they continued to use the Zuni road, as it was the most convenient way to cross the mountain and desert terrain between New Mexico and the west coast. When autos were invented, a wooden plank road was laid on part of the Zuni road, over stretches of sand dunes, and was used by Model T Fords to cross the country. Later the Zuni road was paved and became US Route 66.

"After we cross the river, there is another very old road, a trade route, that all tribes use to travel through the gray desert--Mojave, Yuma and Shoshone country--to the western sea beyond. That road passes through some very dry country. There are few water holes, and they are forty or fifty miles apart. Sometimes bad Yumas and Sohshones and renegade Indians watch the water holes so they can rob and kill travelers who come there. So we will avoid that road.

"After we cross the river, we will travel north and west and into a wide desert valley between two very tall mountain ranges. This valley will lead us north into the country of the Mono Paiutes, the kuzavi eaters, who live by a big salt lake. These people are like brothers to me. There are many marriages between this tribe and my own. My home is in a deep grassy valley high in the mountains to the west. We will rest with the Kuzavi eaters. Then we will climb the mountains and rest with my people." Many Roads spoke as if such a trip on foot through mountains and deserts and hostile Indian country was like a picnic in a garden.

"Don't we need food and water and a tent and other supplies for a trip like that? And maybe a Jeep?" asked Jesse. He could not believe this was happening. Any minute he would surely wake up and find this was all a dream.

"You think like a white man," said Many Roads. "White men travel with strings of horses and mules and wagons to carry all their food and water and every convenience they might need for the whole journey. These burdens make them travel slowly and take longer to cover the distance. They are limited in the roads they can follow. They make a great cloud of dust. It is easy to see them from a distance, and easy to follow their tracks. It is hard for them to hide. If they run out of food they die. A man on foot with no burdens can take any road and cover forty miles in a day. He can travel in ways that leave no tracks. He can easily hide himself. Food and drink are all around us. Food is everywhere. You will see." He picked up one of the rawhide flasks of water from the ground. "This is all we will carry."

Jesse put on his T-shirt and hi-tech sandals and picked up his water flask. He took a purple nylon baseball cap from a pocket of his cargo shorts and put it on. "I guess I'm ready, then," he said. Many Roads was already walking away down the beach. Jesse turned and hurried to catch up. And just like that he was homeward bound. He should have been scared. But somehow he felt at ease with the confidence of Many Roads. And he found himself looking forward to the odyssey ahead.

Chapter Four

As Many Roads and Jesse walked along the shore of the Colorado River, Jesse felt lightness in his chest, and in his step. He was excited and felt a sense of freedom that he had never known before. After they had walked about three miles, they came to a place where a small stream flowed out of a narrow side canyon and into the river. Many Roads turned into the canyon and followed a path alongside the stream. The terrain climbed gently as they moved farther from the river. There were many kinds of flowers, shrubs, cactus and an occasional clump of cottonwood or pinion pine trees. Jesse wore his hi-tech sandals, which were very comfortable for hiking. But Many Roads was barefoot. Yet he seemed to move faster and more comfortably than Jesse.

After walking several miles along the side canyon, Many Roads stopped in a place where a small waterfall about twelve feet high fell from the rocks into a pool. Vegetation was thick in the side canyon. And here by the pool it seemed especially so, like a heavenly garden, a beautiful little grotto, placed in that very spot for the convenience of travelers. Many Roads put all his things on the ground, removed his loincloth and walked naked into the pool until he stood beneath the waterfall. The day was getting warm. The water looked inviting. Jesse stripped naked and followed Many Roads. How refreshing! And what a feeling! This feeling of freedom!

When they left the pool, they stood briefly to let the warm air dry their bodies. As Many Roads replaced his loincloth, Jesse could see that it was a long, narrow strip of soft deerskin, which passed between the legs with the ends brought up and over a braided leather belt and let to hang down, front and rear, almost to the knees. Then Many Roads gathered his things and took a path that ascended the rocky wall on one side of the canyon. Above the waterfall, the canyon widened out, the trail became more sandy, less rocky, easier to walk on. Many Roads stopped by a large manzanita bush, with its glossy red trunk and twisted limbs, covered with small shiny dark-green leaves and brown berries. He began picking and eating berries. He looked at Jesse. "Eat," he said. Jesse began to pick and eat berries, too. They were good.

Many Roads walked over to a round ball-shaped agave plant about two feet tall, with a stalk about 2 inches in diameter growing from its center. The stalk was about five feet tall. Many Roads took his knife from the sheath and with one swift stroke cut the stalk from the plant just above the leaf tips. He quickly inverted the cut stalk, put the cut end to his mouth and drank, then handed the stalk to Jesse. "Drink," he said. Jesse drank some of the liquid from the stalk. It tasted slightly sweet and was very refreshing.

"This is the agave plant. It is also called mescal," said Many Roads. "It grows almost everywhere in the desert. There are many kinds. It can be small as your fist or bigger than a bear. It is an important plant to all Indians, and it has many uses. The leaves are food, the heart is food, the stalk holds drink, a dried stalk is good fire starter, the sharp tips are for sewing, the leaves have fibers to make cord and rope." With that he walked on.

"I guess that's lunch," said Jesse, as he turned and followed Many Roads. They were now well above the canyon bottom, where they had left the river. But they were still down below the rim of the side canyon, the floor of which had begun to slowly rise and widen into a shallow desert valley. They were walking on red rock, sand and shale. There were clumps of thin, short grasses scattered across the terrain, and many small prickly pear cacti. The clumps were small, not much more than ankle high. So Jesse had to watch carefully where he put his feet to avoid getting stuck by their thorns. There was also low growing gray-green sage, mesquite, mescal, manzanita, cottonwood and pinion pine trees. The day was desert hot, he was wet with sweat, but it felt great to be here. Jesse was learning things about himself. He was doing something that his parents and teachers would never permit. They were afraid of everything. They would never believe he was capable of this. He would not have believed it either, if he were not here doing it of necessity. His self-confidence was growing. Though he also realized he could not be doing this without the guidance and assistance of Many Roads.

As the day wore on, the miles fell behind. Jesse was able to appreciate the beauty of the land much more by walking slowly through it than he ever could by whizzing through it in a car or flying over it in an airplane. The desert is hot and harsh. Deserts can be lethal. Deserts everywhere have killed people. But he was learning that the desert can also be a very special place. And not so hostile as he'd always thought. Jesse was very happy and comfortable here.

The high desert valley had gradually become wider and shallower, until they found themselves in flat, open country, with a flat-topped butte rising here and there in the gray hazy distance.

Apache Squaw Harvesting a Small Mescal Plant

The day was getting late, the shadows long. Many roads stopped and was scanning the landscape. "I don't think we will encounter Apaches here. But I want to find an arroyo where we can hide tonight so our fire will not be seen easily across the flat land. It will be cold tonight. A fire will be welcome." He pointed to a cluster of pine trees about a mile distant. "Under those trees there will be wood for a fire, probably an arroyo, and maybe water. A line of trees usually grows along a watercourse, or at a spring or a well. Let's go see."

As they approached the pine trees the sky was doing a light show. Many colors, orange and gold, salmon and crimson, purple, lavender, pink and magenta red, each vied with the others to be brightest. Desert sunsets are intense. Two hundred yards from the trees, Many Roads stopped. "Stay here," he said. Jesse looked at him, uncertain. "Stay here until I return," he repeated. "Don't move or make noise." Jesse did as instructed, and Many Roads moved ahead toward the trees. Jesse lost sight of him, but he stood quietly. Soon Many Roads returned. "It is okay. We are alone. It is smart to approach water holes carefully when you are in dry country," he said. "Predators watch waterholes for prey. Let's go." He hadn't mentioned what kind of predators.

As they approached the trees, Jesse could see that they stood on the edge of a shallow arroyo. There was no water. The watercourse was dry. But the trees were here because there is almost surely ground water not far below the surface. "Gather some of the dry fallen dead wood from under the trees," instructed Many Roads. "I will get rabbits for our dinner." He took an arrow from his quiver. It had no arrowhead, but the wood shaft was shaved to a sharp point. He did not move but stood still surveying the terrain. Then he nocked the arrow, raised the bow, drew and fired. He drew again and another arrow took flight. Then he walked in the direction he had fired, returning in a moment carrying two fat rabbits by their hind feet.

Jesse stood transfixed, watching how easily Many Roads had spotted and procured their dinner. "Gather wood," repeated Many Roads. "Take the wood down in the bottom of the arroyo. That way our fire cannot be seen very far. I will get our breakfast." He tossed the rabbits to the ground and walked back into the brush.

Jesse went to gather the wood. He piled up pieces of dry wood in the arroyo. Soon, Many Roads returned. He tossed to the ground a mescal plant the size of a basketball, a dry mescal stalk, and a small dead sage plant.

As Jesse watched, Many Roads broke up the dry mescal stalk. It was like balsa wood, soft and easily crushed with the fingers. He selected a thick end piece, which he split lengthwise with his knife, laying one half on the ground with the flat side up, to use as a *hearth*. He used the point of his knife to dig a small hole in the center. He sprinkled a pinch of sand in the hole. He crushed another piece of the mescal into crumbs and piled them around the hole. He crushed some dry sage leaves and added them to the pile. He found a stick about half an inch in diameter and a foot and a half long, to use as a *drill*. With his knife he shaved a point on one end. Placing the point of the drill in the hole in the hearth, he spun the stick between the palms of his hands. In a moment a thin line of smoke issued from the pile of tinder. As the smoke increased, Many Roads stopped spinning the stick and began to blow gently into the center of the tinder pile. Quickly a little flame sprouted. He added pieces of the dry mescal stalk, leaning them together with their ends meeting above the flame, like a tiny teepee, and the flame grew. He added small pieces of the dry pine wood, and the flame grew larger. In moments, with found materials, Many Roads had a fire going in the wilderness!

"Find some rocks, about the size of your head," said Many Roads. "Be careful when you pick them up. Scorpions and snakes hide under the stones. Find two rocks with a flat side and big enough to cook a rabbit. Line them up around the fire to get hot." Jesse began to scour the area. While he lined up the stones, Many Roads skinned and gutted the two rabbits, and laid them on top of the flat stones close to the fire. He scraped the skins free of blood and flesh, and spread them flat on the ground, fur side down, placing a few small stones on them to hold them flat.

The evening light show in the sky had passed and it was now dark. The fire was down in the bottom of the arroyo and could not be seen across the flat terrain. Many Roads sat on the earth by the fire and fed some pine sticks into the flames. He pointed to a spot about three feet beyond the fire and said "Dig a small pit about this deep and this much wide," indicating the size with his hands. He took out his knife and began to cut the leaves from the mescal plant. As he dug the pit with a stick of pine, Jesse watched Many Roads trim the leaves from the mescal plant. It was kind of like removing the leaves from an artichoke, to expose the soft heart. But the mescal heart was the size of his head. Many Roads placed the mescal heart on a stone near the fire and began placing the largest of the mescal leaves to roast on the stones near the fire.

"We traveled about thirty miles today," said Many Roads. "Maybe two more days will take us to the Zuni road, and another two days to the river. Until we reach the river we will drink mescal and save our water as much as possible. If we find waterholes, we can drink our fill." He reached out to turn and re-position the rabbit and the mescal leaves. "Food and drink are all around us. There is no reason to hurry. But with need we can increase the miles we walk in a day." Jesse would be happy to keep it at thirty, or less. But he kept silent.

Suddenly, a wild fluttering sound issued from the air above them! Jesse ducked reflexively and threw up his arms in defense! Many Roads laughed. "Quail," he said. "They are attracted to the firelight after sunset. If we want them for food, we can knock them down by throwing sticks. But tonight we eat rabbit and mescal."

They sat in the desert night staring quietly into the fire. The aroma of wood smoke and roasting rabbit filled Jesse's nostrils. He was starved after the long day's walk. Many Roads continued to turn the rabbit and the mescal leaves. When the food was cooked, Many Roads handed Jesse a roasted mescal leaf. "Eat the wide thick part. I did not remove the fibers along the edges. The fibers are attached to the sharp spine at the tip. Break the tip and peel the fibers away." He ate one himself and tossed the tip and fibers into the fire. Jesse followed suit. The leaves were thick and fleshy, with a mild sweet flavor.

Many Roads took up another mescal leaf, broke the tip and peeled the fibers away. With thumb and fingers of one hand he stripped the flesh from the strands of fiber. "The mescal leaf tip can also be used for sewing," he said. He held up the sharp tip with long fibers attached. It was a needle with a cluster of threads already attached and ready for sewing! Holding the sharp tip in one hand, he draped the group of fibers over one thigh and with the palm of the other hand rolled the fibers back and forth, creating a coarse cord depending from the sharp point, ready for sewing!

When they had consumed one rabbit and the mescal leaves, Many Roads said "We will save the other rabbit for our breakfast with the mescal heart." He rose and walked into the darkness, returning with an armload of green leafy plant material. One by one, he used a pine stick to roll half of the hot stones surrounding the fire ring into the adjacent pit Jesse had excavated. He placed the trimmed mescal heart on top of the hot rocks, then carefully laid a thick layer of the greenery on top. He laid the flat hot stones on top and covered the entire pit and its contents with the sand that had come out of the hole. "In the morning this will be finished cooking and will make a good hot morning meal. If you get cold in the night, sleep on top of this spot. It will stay warm all night."

Jesse propped himself against the sloped wall of the arroyo, with his feet to the fire, clasped his hands behind his head, and looked up at the stars. He could see the Milky Way, curving and stretching away. And he saw himself as a bug on the Earth, and the Earth as just another tiny speck lost at the remote end of that spinning reach of stars. His eyes closed and he was sound asleep.

Chapter Five

Jesse woke sore and stiff, partly from the previous day's thirty miles and partly from sleeping on the hard ground. The fire had gone out. Many Roads was gone. Jesse stood, stretched and yawned. Early morning chill was on the air. He squatted and held his hand over the ashes of the fire, feeling to see if there were any hot coals left, wondering if there would be enough to re-start the fire. Many Roads appeared then and said "No fire," as if he had read Jesse's thoughts. "In the daylight the smoke can be seen for many miles. We will be careful until we are in more familiar country."

"You are not familiar with this country? You have not been here before? Is this Apache country?" asked Jesse.

"Only one time before," said Many Roads. "First time was when I came here. Not exactly the same route. This is the far edge of Apache country. They have no reason to come here."

"Do you ever get lost?" asked Jesse.

"I am not lost. You are lost, white boy," replied Many Roads, shaking his head.

Jesse ignored the remark. "You never lose your way when you travel in places you've never been?" he asked.

"No. I use my eyes to study the land. Water flows downhill; desert is different from mountains. I ask other Indian people about trails and conditions, about water and food. I use my knowledge and experience. I do not lose my way," said Many Roads, mildly annoyed by the questions. "I am here," he said, tapping his chest with his knuckles. "I can go anywhere. Never lost. Home is here," he said, tapping his chest again. "If home is inside you, how can you be lost?" This was a new idea to Jesse.

Last night's rabbit was still lying on the stones. With his hands, Many Roads carefully uncovered the pit containing the mescal heart. He removed sand and flat stones, the layers of leaves, and then the mescal heart. He set the heart on one of the flat stones by the fire, took out his knife and sliced off a piece, which he handed to Jesse. He sliced off another for himself and took a bite. Jesse followed suit. It was hot, and soft, and tasty, with a mild nutty flavor and a meaty texture similar to artichoke hearts, without the oil and vinegar.

Many Roads picked up the rabbit, tore off a leg and handed it to Jesse, tore off another for himself. The food was good. The setting and ambience could be no better. Jesse had always thought of the desert as a barren, hostile place. But he was beginning to see that it not only held an abundance of food, but a great variety as well. And there are also a huge variety of flowers. The desert is a beautiful garden.

After they finished the food, Many Roads found a milkweed plant with long thin stalks. He selected a stalk, cut it from the plant, laid it on a rock and pounded the entire length with a stick. Then holding an end in one hand, he pulled the crushed stalk through the thumb and fingers of the other hand several times, stripping away the crushed plant material and leaving a long bunch of fibers, thin as hair. These he laid across his thigh and with the flat of one hand rolled them back and forth, until he had a coarse cord about three feet long. He rolled up the two rabbit pelts and tied them with the cord, and then hung them on his belt. "You can also use milkweed or the hemp plant to make string or rope," said Many Roads. "These pelts will make a nice gift to others we might visit on our way." With that he picked up his bow, stood still and surveyed the campsite for a moment, then climbed out of the arroyo and began the day's walk.

The day passed much like the previous day. Though, the terrain was different. As the miles flowed past, Jesse noticed changes in the land. First he noticed that the color of the sand and rock was fading from red to pink. Then he began to notice the appearance of small barrel cactus, and cholla cactus, with thin lumpy arms, dark glossy green, with long yellow spines. And there were more kinds of prickly pear cactus, some of them much larger than the ones he had seen so far. Many had red or purple fruit on their pear shaped leaves.

About midday, Many Roads saw a line of greenery in the distance. He pointed. "Water," he said. They shifted their line of travel slightly to aim for the trees. When they reached the trees, they found pines and cottonwoods, and a small stream. They found a small pool, where they drank their fill. They had used some of the water in their flasks, so they refilled them. The pool was not big enough to swim in. But they were able to splash themselves and wet their heads and faces. Many Roads pointed to a round animal track in the wet sand near the water's edge. "Puma," he said. Jesse realized suddenly that in the wilderness everybody is on the menu, including himself.

Refreshed, they continued their trek. Soon after they left the water, Many Roads spotted another manzanita bush. It was loaded with the same brown berries they had eaten yesterday. They picked and ate berries until they were satisfied, then continued on their way. They covered more than thirty miles that day. Jesse noticed that Many Roads often looked back, the way they had come, and a few times he stopped and surveyed their rear trail for several minutes before continuing. That afternoon, Many Roads spied some trees that indicated the possibility of water, and decided to stop earlier than on the previous day. When they arrived at the trees, there was a dry arroyo. "Gather wood and put it in the arroyo," said Many Roads. "Make more wood tonight. The puma is following. I will get rabbits."

When Jesse had a nice pile of firewood stacked up, Many Roads returned with two rabbits, which he tossed on the ground by the firewood. "Come," he said. "I will show you how to make a fire." Jesse followed.

Many Roads climbed from the arroyo and began to look around. He found a dead dry agave plant and took the stalk in his hand. "Find a dead agave, like this one. The stalk is soft, you can crush it with your hand. It makes good fire starter. You can find them everywhere." As he spoke he broke off the stalk, then squeezed his hand and crushed part of the stalk to crumbs.

Then he walked a few feet away to a dry sage plant. He indicated the dead dry leaves and stripped off a handful, which he displayed in his open palm. He crushed them to show their dryness. "The dry sage leaves also make good fire starter. It will catch with the smallest spark and continue to glow until it is all burned up." He took up the agave stalk and a branch from the dead sage bush, returned to the arroyo, and deposited them by the firewood. He found a straight stick to use for a drill. "We will wait for darkness. Then you will start the fire," he said. He handed the drill stick to Jesse and said "Shave a point on one end." He drew his knife and offered it hilt first to Jesse. "This stick is manzanita. Any hardwood is good for the drill stick. Use soft wood for the hearth if there is no agave."

"I have a knife," Jesse remembered! He drew a Swiss army knife from a pocket of his cargo shorts. Many Roads leaned forward, looking closely. Jesse folded open the blade.

"That is a knife?" asked Many Roads. "It might peel a manzanita berry!"

His feelings a little hurt, Jesse said defensively "It has other tools, too." Many Roads watched as Jesse opened the screwdriver blade, the Phillips screwdriver, the scissors, the corkscrew, and the awl. He pulled tweezers out of the end of the knife.

"You need a knife," repeated Many Roads.

Jesse closed all the blades except the large blade. He took the drill stick and shaved a point on one end. "Good," said Many Roads. "Come." Again he climbed from the arroyo and walked away into the brush. Jesse followed. Soon Many Roads stopped and indicated a clump of prickly pear cactus. These had round red fruit at the tip of each pear shaped leaf. The leaves were flat, about an inch thick and ten inches across, pale green in color, with a shape somewhat like that of a pear, with clusters of short, pale spines scattered across the leaf surface. The fruits were about the size and shape of a large plum, several of them on the tip of each leaf, red to purple in color.

"This is cactus fruit, very good to eat. But the surface of the fruit is covered with tiny spines, like fuzz, too small to see. If you touch, they stick in your skin and feels like a burn from fire. This can last two days. So we first put them in the fire and burn off the spines. We roast the fruit a little bit, too. Then eat." He took his knife and slashed off two large pear shaped leaves, each holding several fruits at the tip. They fell on the ground. He took his knife and speared one leaf and picked it up and walked away toward the arroyo. Jesse opened his Swiss Army knife, speared the other and followed.

They sat on the rim of the arroyo watching the sunset evening light show. Jesse was getting used to this freedom stuff, and the self-confidence that was growing in him. "You said the puma is following us. Are you sure?" asked Jesse, a little concerned.

"Yes," replied Many Roads.

"What can we do?" asked Jesse.

"We wait. And keep sharp eyes," replied Many roads. "The puma always hunts from behind. He follows. When he finds an opportunity he attacks the prey from behind, and bites the back of the neck. This way he can hold the prey until he can break the neck or work his grip around to the throat. He always hunts this way. Or sometimes, if he is very hungry, or sick or old, he will come at night, into your house, while you sleep. I have been watching for a way to kill this one before it's dark, so I can see what to shoot at." Many Roads took the knife and sheath from his belt and handed it to Jesse. "You keep this. You need a knife. If the puma gets you in his grip, fight back. Try to get the knife in his soft belly. Hit him with rocks, or your fist. He is a coward and will run if you fight. If you run, he will chase and bite your neck."

"Now you don't have a knife," observed Jesse.

"I have my bow. And I know how to fight him better than you do," said Many Roads. "Keep the knife. It is a gift. I can make another."

"Thank you," said Jesse. It was a beautiful black obsidian blade, about five inches long, by two inches wide at the hilt, with a rawhide wrapped handle, in a stiff rawhide sheath. "Thank you," Jesse repeated.

Once the evening light was almost gone, Many Roads said "You start a fire now."

"I'm not sure I can," said Jesse.

"Do as you saw me do yesterday," said Many Roads.

Jesse tried to remember. He took the dry mescal stalk, broke off a thick piece, crushed it with his heel, selected a thick piece. He used his new knife to split it into two halves, took one piece and gouged a hole in the center, then laid it down and piled flakes of the crushed agave stalk and dry sage leaves on it. He added a pinch of sand to the pile of tinder, without knowing why. He remembered that Many Roads had done so. Then he removed a Bic lighter from a pocket of his shorts and lit the tinder. As the flame grew he added pieces of pine. Many Roads laughed. "What will you do when your fire shooter stops working?" he asked. Jesse thought he had a point. It might be good to know how to do it the Indian way.

Jesse did manage to start the fire. He was very proud of himself. Even though he had to use his lighter. Once it was going, Many Roads began skinning and gutting the rabbits. "Find some flat stones to lay the rabbits on," he said. He treated the skins as before. Jesse placed two flat stones close to the flames and tilted them inward a little bit, and Many Roads laid the rabbits on them to cook. Then he cut one cactus fruit from its pear shaped leaf, speared it with the fire drill, and held it in the flames. Then he handed the stick to Jesse, with a gesture toward the fire. He picked up another pine stick and shaved a point on the end. He cut another cactus fruit from its leaf, speared it and held it in the fire. When the fruits were cooked, they ate, holding them on the sticks, like two boys with candy apples at the county fair. The cactus fruit tasted both sweet and slightly tart, with the fleshy texture of a plum. "Mmmm, that's good," remarked Jesse.

Suddenly, Many Roads grabbed his bow and nocked an arrow, in one swift, fluid move. Jesse saw a shadow on the rim of the arroyo just as it launched itself. He ducked, raised his arms to shield his head, heard the deep twang of the bowstring in his ear, and the puma fell dead right on top of him, with Many Roads' arrow through his heart.

Jesse screamed. He screamed again and again. His breathing stopped. Many Roads pulled the cougar off of Jesse and stretched its body on the earth beyond the fire. Jesse stopped screaming. "You can breathe again," said Many Roads, nudging Jesse with his toe. "The puma is dead." Now Jesse started breathing again, gasping, greedily sucking in lungs full of oxygen. Then he was retching.

Many Roads resumed his seat by the fire, picked up a rabbit, pulled off a leg and offered it to Jesse, who shook his head. "Let me finish hurling first, would you?" he growled. He was not hungry any more. Many Roads began to eat the rabbit leg.

Jesse was calming down. He was embarrassed by his panic attack. He looked at the cougar. The arrow struck the heart and killed the animal while he was still in the air! A masterful shot that probably saved his life. This Indian boy, his same age, was his own master. He had the courage and skills to live and travel alone in the wilderness and be at home there. And now after being stalked and attacked by a wild, man-eating mountain lion, he had killed the predator, saved Jesse's life and his own, and was now calmly finishing his dinner, as though nothing extraordinary had happened!

Jesse finally calmed down enough to help Many Roads finish eating the rabbit and cactus fruit.

Chapter Six

When Jesse woke the next morning, Many Roads was busy scraping the flesh and blood from the skin side of the cougar hide. He had already skinned and gutted the animal. The carcass was hanging in one of the pinion pines, where Many Roads had hung it to make the work of skinning easier. Now Many Roads had the cougar skin draped over a boulder and was busy with the scraping. Now that Jesse was awake, Many Roads set his work aside and stood. "Come," he said. "We have something for breakfast that is good with cold rabbit." Jesse followed as Many Roads walked away and into the brush.

In a large, clear space that was open and free of brush, he stopped. "Look closely," he said, pointing at the ground. Jesse saw bare ground, sand and shale, and an occasional sparse tuft of thin grass. Nothing else. Many Roads stooped and brought his fingertip close to a small pale colored stem, about an inch tall and thick as a wooden matchstick. Then Jesse saw more of them. They had no leaf or flower. They were not very obvious, but once you saw them, dozens and then hundreds more of them became apparent, scattered across the bare earth, sticking up out of the sand and shale. Many Roads used a stick to dig up one of the sprouts. The root was a small, light brown tuber about the size of a peanut. He brushed off the dirt and popped it into his mouth, dug up another and offered it to Jesse, who brushed it off and tasted. In all ways it was exactly like a sweet potato, crisp and crunchy, starchy, very sweet and tasty, with a hint of chocolate. The two boys dug up a quantity that filled Jesse's baseball cap and returned to the fire, where they enjoyed a breakfast of cold rabbit and raw sweet potatoes.

Many Roads returned to his work scraping the cougar skin. "This puma skin will make a fine gift," he said. "And we have four rabbit pelts. Rabbits are important to all Indians. We eat more rabbit meat than all other kinds of meat combined. Rabbits are abundant, they are everywhere. And the skins are useful for making blankets and warm clothing. The skins are small and not very strong. So we have a method that makes them useable. We take the skins and cut them into strips about two inches wide, and sew them together end to end, to make very long strips. Then we twist the strips, so the skin turns in and the soft fur turns outward, making a long furry rope. Then we weave these long furry ropes into blankets, very soft and warm. Or we make capes and robes for winter clothing." (see p. 18)

He worked in silence for a while. Then: "A young Indian man shares a teepee with other unmarried men and boys," said Many Roads. "He has no house of his own. Everything he hunts is given to others. Not until he takes a wife does he have his own house or hunt for himself. Then he keeps the bear and puma and sheep skins he kills for rugs and beds in his own teepee. He keeps the meat he hunts. If he hunts more than he needs, he shares it with those who have no one to hunt for them. I will give this puma skin to my mother's sister when we reach Mono Lake. Her man was killed on a hunt. She has no son."

When he was finished, he rolled up the rabbit pelts inside the cougar pelt and tied it with agave cord. He looked at the cougar carcass hanging in the tree. "My tribe does not eat the meat from scavengers: the puma or coyote or wolf or vulture," he said. He walked over to the tree, reached up and cut the cord, letting the carcass fall to the earth. "I will leave him for the scavengers." Then he replaced the knife in its sheath and handed it to Jesse. "I borrowed your knife while you slept," he smiled. Jesse accepted the knife and attached it to his belt.

When they were ready for the day's walk, Jesse suggested that they dig up more sweet potatoes to carry with them. "Carry as many as you like," responded Many Roads. "I prefer to go without the burden. When I grow hungry, I will find food. That is the Indian way."

They struck out southwest once more, heading for the Zuni road. Around midday, Many Roads stopped and pointed to a row of jagged black hills in the distance. "I have heard that those hills are a place to find good stone for knives and arrow points," he said. "It is not far from our path. Let's go there and see."

Their path had veered now and then, making twists and turns to stay in the flat terrain and skirt the buttes and ridges that stood up from the flat land. As they walked, the miles flowed past, and Jesse noticed more changes in the landscape. The color of the sand and rocks continued to fade from pink to gray. The barrel cactus grew larger and more varieties became evident. He began to see Joshua trees, a kind of yucca that grows in the form of a contorted tree, with globular tufts of the long, pointed yucca leaves at the ends of the branches. Jesse could see that they would reach the hills that Many Roads was aiming for well before dark.

When they arrived at the foot of the hills, they chose a campsite in a gully, hidden in a stand of desert pine trees. There was plenty of firewood, no water. "Gather wood," said Many Roads. "I will get rabbits." He disappeared up the gully and Jesse began to pile up the night's firewood. He had finished his task and was sitting on a boulder at the base of a pine tree on the rim of the gully gazing across the landscape, savoring the beauty and the quiet of this place. In a city it is not possible to ever hear it so quiet. A city is always humming and buzzing with nervous energy, never silent, never still. If you enjoy bedlam, you should be happy in a city. If you desire peace and quiet, you must seek it in the country. You can't have it both ways. He was beginning to realize that he has a choice.

Many Roads returned with two rabbits. And he had found the stone he was seeking. He removed the wildcat fur pouch from his shoulder and emptied it on the ground. It contained several dozen shards of obsidian, a stone that looks like glass, often black but sometimes red or other colors. "For arrow points," he said, as he emptied the bag. "This stone makes the best arrow points, spear points and knives." Also in the bag was a tip from a deer antler, about six inches long, a patch of thick leather, roughly nine inches across, and a small bundle of rawhide lace. Also, there were the claws from the cougar. "Claws from the puma or leopard have strength and power. If you kill them, you wear some of the claws. And with other claws you can make a totem for your teepee, or your spear. These are tokens of the power you inherit when you kill a big cat, or a bear, marking you as a fierce warrior. You took his life, now his strength is in you. As you grow older, the numbers of your rugs and your totems of power increase. On seeing you, your enemies will turn and run in fear! At least this is the theory."

In his hand, Many Roads carried five larger pieces of the obsidian, each between six and nine inches long, two or more inches wide and a quarter of an inch thick. As he displayed the stones, he said "Now that I gave my knife to you, I must make another for myself, so I won't need to keep borrowing yours." As he spoke, he laid the leather patch on his thigh, laid an eight inch piece of the black stone on the leather pad and, holding the stone with his left hand, he began to chip small flakes from one edge, using the tip of the antler in his right hand to press on the brittle edge.

As he worked, the shape of a knife blade quickly began to emerge. It was straight along the back, and curved from tip to hilt along the sharp cutting edge. The blade was about six inches long, and two inches wide at the hilt. From the hilt it narrowed into a short tang. By sundown, he had the rough shape of the knife chipped. "The knife you're making has a much shorter handle than the one you gave me," noticed Jesse.

"Yes," replied Many Roads. "Your knife has a stone handle, wrapped in rawhide. For this knife I will make a bone handle. I will kill a deer or antelope tomorrow. I will take a leg bone or piece of antler for my knife handle. The knee joint makes an attractive pommel. Do you think you can start the fire and skin the rabbits, tonight? So I can keep working on my knife?"

"Good question," answered Jesse. He rose and went through the motions of making the fire the Indian way. But he could not get the faintest wisp of smoke to rise from the tinder, no matter how hard he spun the drill. Finally, out of frustration, he brought forth the Bic lighter and had the fire going quickly.

Then he found rocks to lay the rabbits on and placed them close to the fire. He got out his Swiss Army knife to skin the rabbits, since he judged the small blade would work better at this task than the larger stone knife. He picked up a rabbit and made the cuts he had seen Many Roads make, then peeled the skin off the carcass, like turning a sock inside out. He sliced open the body cavity and removed the entrails, then laid the rabbit on the rocks to cook. He repeated the process with the other rabbit, then scraped the flesh and blood from the skin sides of the pelts and spread them fur side down on the ground, using a few small stones to hold them flat, as he had seen Many Roads do. "I will find some cactus fruit," he said, picking up two pine sticks to use for spearing.

"The potatoes were good this morning," suggested Many Roads. "If you look for them, you may find some here."

"That sounds good, too," said Jesse. "Let's see what I can find." He left Many Roads in the gully chipping his knife. As he looked for signs of sweet potatoes or a nice clump of prickly pear with fruit, he felt very pleased with himself and the contributions he was able to make by gathering wood, building the fire and finding food. He found a likely clump of prickly pear and cut off two large ears, each with several fruits at the tip. He shaved points on his two sticks and speared the ears to carry back to the fire.

He sat down next to Many Roads, to watch him work on the knife. He cut off and speared a cactus fruit to roast in the fire. As he worked, Many Roads spoke, "We are close to the Zuni road. We will find it early tomorrow. Two more days and we will reach the river. There is a Mojave village where we can stay, and maybe eat Mojave food. The Mojaves are large people, tall and heavy, friendly and good-natured, not aggressive or acquisitive. They cultivate crops like the Mexicans and whites, corn and pumpkins, squash and beans. We will eat and sleep with them. I will try to kill a deer or antelope when we get close, for a gift."

Jesse tended to cooking the rabbits. When they were ready the boys ate rabbit and cactus fruit for their supper. Many Roads continued working on his knife. He was still working on the knife when Jesse fell asleep beside the fire beneath a sky thick with stars.

Pots & Baskets

Chapter Seven

Next morning after breakfast, they once more struck out southwest and, as Many Roads had predicted, they found the Zuni road before morning was gone. Jesse had wondered if they would find it at all. It was just a dirt track across hundreds of miles of empty Arizona desert. How could you possibly expect to find it? But when you saw it, it was hard to imagine how you could miss it, this ancient highway of sand crossing the desert wilderness.

They turned west and began to follow the Zuni Road. It was much easier to walk on than the desert terrain, since it was wide and smooth and clear of cactus, brush and stone. The first day on the Zuni road the walking was much easier than across the desert, and the miles flowed past more quickly. They relaxed their pace and still covered thirty miles that day.

The pink color continued to fade and by the end of the day was almost gone from the land. The sand and shale had turned mostly gray by now, and Joshua trees had become so numerous that this might be called a forest. Can you call cactus a forest? Here and there in the distance, the hills that stood up were no longer flat-topped buttes, like those nearer the Grand Canyon, but were jagged and sharp, like rows of ragged, broken teeth. And the colors of the hills were different here, darker and richer, black and indigo, purple and maroon.

They camped alongside the road that night. As they began their second day on the Zuni road, Many Roads said "I would like to reach the river before dark today. Can you run?"

"I can try," replied Jesse. "How far? What do you have in mind?"

"If we run as much as we are able all day," said Many Roads, "We can make it to the river before dark. There are many trees near the water, plenty of wood, good places to camp, with fresh water, good cover for deer and antelope, good cover for you and me. Run until you can run no more. Then we will walk until you recover. Then run some more." With that he took off at a trot, and Jesse followed. Every day, in every way, Many Roads and this trek were stretching Jesse. And he was loving every minute of it.

They ran and recovered, ran and recovered, all day long. They stopped for a lunch on manzanita berries, then continued their marathon run. They ran through the Joshua tree forest toward the dusty orange ball of the sun as it slowly sank lower in the western sky. Finally they came within sight of a line of trees in the distance that marked the river. Shrubs and trees of many kinds grew thicker and taller as they approached the water. A wide area of vegetation, a veritable jungle of desert plants and trees, lined both sides of the river. Many Roads slowed to a walk. "Walk quietly, now," he said. "Look for deer or antelope."

As the evening sky began its fierce sunset performance, they reached the river, the brilliant colors reflected in the water's surface. The Zuni road ended on a broad flat beach, at water's edge. The river here was perhaps a quarter mile wide, lazy and slow. It did not seem like the same wild river he had ridden in the raft. The river mirrored the many-colored sunset sky. Many Roads turned north and continued walking along the shore. Soon they reached a place where a small stream flowed into the river. "We camp here," said Many Roads. They both dropped to the sand and drank from the stream. "Find firewood and make a fire. No need to hide. This is Mojave lands," said Many Roads. "I will look for food." He followed the stream away from the river into the brush and trees.

When Many Roads returned he carried two fat rabbits, which he laid down by the fire. "Many tracks by this stream," he said, "Tracks of deer and antelope, coyote, quail, dove, wildcat, fox, raccoon, turkey. Many animals live here, by the water. In the morning I will find a deer or antelope for a gift to the Mojave people. Their village is not far." He picked up one rabbit and began skinning. Jesse picked up the other and followed suit, pleased that he knew how.

"There are many cactus fruits here. Shall we have some with our rabbit?" said Many Roads.

"Sounds good," replied Jesse. This still seemed like a dream to Jesse. He hoped he would not wake up for awhile yet. He was enjoying this.

As they sat feeding the fire and cooking rabbit and cactus fruit, Many Roads suddenly exploded into action. Leaping to his feet, he grabbed his bow and nocked an arrow, leapt twelve feet away from the fire in two strides, spun and knelt with bow drawn. Jesse was startled, his breath stopped, his throat caught. He looked in the direction the bow was pointing and saw two Indians, tall muscular warriors with bows and spears and knives. They stood looking quietly at Many Roads for a moment, then vanished, fading silently into the night. Jesse turned to look at Many Roads, but he was gone, too, without a sound.

The entire event took no more than two or three seconds. Now it was finished, and Jesse's heart was pounding in his chest. He found himself on his feet, knife in hand, crouched and ready to defend himself. But everyone was gone, there was no one here to fight with, he was alone.

Then after a few minutes Many Roads returned to the circle of firelight, to find Jesse still on his feet, still holding his unsheathed knife. "Very good," he said, as he sat down by the fire.

Jesse sheathed his knife and sat back down. "What just happened?" he asked. "Who were they?"

"I was caught with my guard down," Many Roads replied. "They were Yumas. Not friendly. Troublesome. Treacherous. Sometimes they rob or kill. I did not expect to see any Indians here but Mojaves. Their village is very close. A few steps beyond the stream and we would be camping in their gardens. It is unusual to find Yumas so close to the Mojave village. Their territory is farther south and west. I think they were surprised to find us here, as well. The Mojaves do not carry weapons. Seeing me with my drawn bow startled and confused them. It was good for you to follow my action by drawing your knife. They approached our fire expecting to find unarmed Mojaves. Instead they found a Paiute and a white man, armed and ready to fight. They are known to be cowards. I followed them, more than half a mile. They were moving away at a run and speaking in excited voices. I do not think they will return tonight."

Chapter Eight

Next morning, after a breakfast of cold rabbit, Many Roads walked into the brush and returned immediately with several branches from a dead manzanita. He chose two forked pieces, which he trimmed to resemble deer antlers. He tied them to his head with the leather strap from his water bottle, to impersonate a male deer. "You stay here," he said. "The deer will think I am one of them. I know where they are. I can get very close. This will not take long." He turned and disappeared into the brush.

Jesse sat on the beach beside the stream, looking across the river. He could probably swim it. Many Roads probably could, as well. But their clothes would get wet. No big deal. But he did not know if it was okay to get Many Roads' bow and arrows wet, or the furs. They now had the cougar skin and eight rabbit pelts. Maybe the Mojaves would loan them a canoe.

In the daylight he could see that there were more trees in the greenbelt along the riverbank than he had seen in the dim evening light when they arrived. There were many more big trees than he had yet seen, junipers and desert pines and cottonwoods and willows, and palm trees, too. Maybe these were date palms. Jesse loved dates.

Jesse found himself getting used to a different way of relating to time. Here in the wilderness time was unimportant, did not have any purpose. There were no appointments, no deadlines, no need to be anywhere or to accomplish anything, no demands or constraints, beyond his immediate needs for food, fire and shelter. And learning to meet those needs was a welcome challenge. He had a growing sense that he was living in a huge garden, where there is always something to eat and drink, always some place to take shelter, or things to make shelter with, always things to make fire with. Living in a garden is a nice idea, when you think about it. And learning how to live in harmony with and be part of the garden, to take all your needs from the garden, is a thrill. Maybe we are living in Heaven. Maybe it's just a matter of perspective.

There were no rules here, no itineraries. He could go where he chose or do as he pleased, whenever he pleased. He had never felt this way before. His whole life, from his earliest memory, had been scheduled and planned, down to the minute, and governed by rules and more rules. His mom already had his college picked out and had been sending them stuff and making phone calls, since before he was even in high school. His whole life had been planned, before he was even born, and he had not been asked for input. It bothered him sometimes. But he didn't know any other way.

But none of that seemed important here in the desert hundreds of miles from a road or a city. Jesse had begun to feel like he was a part of this place, part of the land, he felt that he had a role to play in the drama of life that was unfolding here at every moment. He felt a sense of belonging. He felt at home here.

Many Roads returned. "I shot a deer and two turkeys," he said. "There is a Mojave village very near. Look around for a straight pole to carry the deer. I will make string to tie up the legs."

"Sure," said Jesse

Neither had mentioned the Indian visitors of last night. Jesse quickly found a suitable pole, and Many Roads produced some stout milkweed cords. The boys gathered up their things, and Jesse followed Many Roads into the brush to find the deer. It was lying on the sand where it had fallen, not far from the stream. Many Roads tied the front feet together, then the rear feet. They slipped the pole between the legs, and Jesse stooped to pick up an end of the carrying pole. "Wait," said Many Roads. "There are two turkeys, also." He brought the turkeys and tied their feet to the middle of the pole that held the deer. "That's it. We are ready now," said Many Roads.

They made their way out of the brush to the river, then they crossed the stream northward toward the Mojave village. On the opposite bank they spotted a well-worn path going in the direction of the village.

The Mojave village was less than a mile north of the stream. At about half a mile, through brush and cattails and tall grasses, they suddenly came out into the Mojave vegetable gardens, large tracts of pumpkins, melons, squash, corn and beans. The gardens extended from the river's edge inland about half a mile. In the distance, half a mile north beyond the vegetable garden, they could see the stick and grass huts of the village, very similar to the Chemahuevi houses, but more of them. The path they followed was one of several well-used pathways that criss-crossed the gardens. Women and children worked naked in the morning sun. Teenage Mojave boys could be seen at intervals along the perimeter of the gardens, lookouts posted to keep the deer and antelopes away. Those animals that approached too close would become prey to these eager young hunters.

As they drew close to the village, Many Roads was recognized and several men formed a welcoming committee at the garden's edge. This village was much larger than the Chemahuevi village in the Grand Canyon. This village had maybe a hundred brush houses and a population of four or five hundred.

"Many Roads!" called the chief, raising a hand in greeting.

"Chief Pumpkin Eater!" replied Many Roads, raising a hand in return.

As they drew close, "It is always good to see you, my friend!" called out Many Roads.

"I am always happy to see **you**, my young friend!" returned the chief.

"I am returning to my village in the mountains," said Many Roads. I have brought this nice deer and a pair of fat turkeys to share one more feast with my friend before I depart your country."

The chief was clearly happy to see Many Roads, treating him with the respect of one of the older men, or of a favorite son. He signaled two young men to take the deer and turkeys from Many Roads and Jesse. "We will have a feast tonight, and singing and dancing, in your honor!" said Chief Pumpkin Eater.

Jesse observed the Mojave men to be six feet tall and more, strong, athletic and well muscled. They wore their hair long and loose down their back to the waist, not braided or tied. They all wore a soft leather loincloth, like Many Roads, and were barefoot, even the chief. This seemed like the popular desert fashion.

The women looked much like the men. They, too, were tall, lean, long-limbed, athletic and well-muscled. Some wore their hair long and loose, like the men; others gathered and tied the hair in a bun or ponytail, at the back of the neck. Many wore the leather loincloth, like the men, while some wore short leather skirts and others went naked.

Many Roads enjoyed feasting with the Mojaves. They were happy people who needed no reason for a celebration. And they always prepared interesting foods that Many Roads had never eaten before. He and Jesse went to the river to bathe and take a nap on the shore. When they woke they saw several Mojave boys fishing in the river. They were using fish hooks made of cactus thorns, heated in fire and bent to the shape of a hook. Agave or hemp fibers made the line. The boys had a string of a dozen fat fish lying on the beach, their contribution to the feast. Many Roads and Jesse returned to the village rested and refreshed, to find the villagers hustling and bustling everywhere, preparing for the evening feast.

Many Roads found the chief and asked for the return of one of the leg bones from his deer to use for the handle of his new knife. The chief offered, in lieu of a leg bone, a piece of deer antler that he had chosen and already shaped for use as a knife handle. It only needed to have a blade fitted and set into it. Many Roads accepted the offer.

A hut was made available for the boys' use. It was positioned at the edge of the village on a slight rise that enjoyed a view above and across most of the village, to the gardens beyond and the river curving away in the distance. Many Roads sat down in the shade of the hut, brought out his wildcat fur pouch. He removed his tools and began chipping his knife. "Can you swim?" asked Many Roads.

"Yes," answered Jesse.

"Can you swim across the river?" asked Many Roads.

"Easily," replied Jesse. "Across and back, pulling you in a boat!" He was not really bragging. He felt he did not exaggerate by much, in case Many Roads challenged him to prove his words. Swimming was his sport. He did well in competition and had won medals. His high school coach wanted him to prepare for the Olympics. But Jesse did not think he would be happy devoting so much of himself to athletic competition. Though, he hoped to win a college scholarship by swimming.

Many Roads laughed. "You won't have to do that," he said. "I just wanted to know if you are a swimmer. Tomorrow we will cut bundles of reeds, tie them with hemp cord and make boats. We can cross the river when we depart without getting our food and other things wet. We will leave the boats on the far bank for the Mojaves.

Then Jesse noticed the skins were missing from among their gear. "The skins are not here," he remarked. "The cougar and rabbit skins. Do you know where they are?"

"They are being cleaned and dressed," replied Many Roads. "Our host offered to have the work done for me while we are here, and I am happy to accept his offer. They have a good place to work on skins. And the deer brain is fresh. To dress the skins and make them soft, we rub the brain from the animal all over the surface of the skin. It is much easier to do it here than on the trail. And it takes a few days."

As they spoke, a woman arrived with melon so ripe and sweet its perfume announced its coming. She held a round earthenware bowl, filled with melon slices of several kinds and colors. The melons were perfectly vine ripe. Melons don't get better than this. And both boys were partial to melon.

The hut was furnished with two beds of dry grass, covered with soft tanned deerskins. There was a rolled up rabbit skin blanket on each bed. And sitting on the earth was a large water jug, made of a dry gourd with a narrow waist, and a rope tied around the waist, with a carrying loop handle. There was a fire laid on the ground in front of the hut, ready to start, and a small pile of firewood nearby. The accommodations were simple, and primitive. Yet this was true hospitality.

Chapter Nine

By the time the evening sunset had begun, Many Roads had finished his knife. He had carved into the end of the antler handle a cavity perfectly fitted to receive the short tang at the end of the stone blade. He had acquired a lump of pine pitch, which he worked into a thin disc about two inches across. Warm and pliable, this was folded over the butt end of the tang and pressed tight to the surface of the stone. Then the blade was fitted and pressed hard into the antler handle. Then he used some soft rawhide lacing that had been soaking in water, to wrap tightly around and around the end of the antler handle for about an inch, binding it to the stone blade. The final end of the lace was passed under the last wrap, cinched up tight, and trimmed. The excess pitch was trimmed away. The knife was finished! And a beautiful knife it was, too, striking in its simplicity of design, made from the most common of materials.

"As the rawhide lace dries, it shrinks," explained Many Roads. "This tightens the grip of the antler against the stone blade. A knife like this will last many years. This is a very good way to make a knife." He put his hand into the wildcat fur pouch and brought out a small object, which he tossed to Jesse. "For you," he said. Jesse caught the object and examined it. It was one of the cougar claws. A hole had been made through the fat end of the claw, a soft leather thong passed through the hole, and the ends of the thong knotted. He noticed that Many Roads now wore one around his own neck.

"Put it on," said Many Roads. "You share the credit. You should have an emblem of power. I shot him in the air, you caught him before he hit the ground." Their eyes met, and they both laughed. Jesse placed the loop of thong over his head and let the cougar claw rest on his chest. "From an event like this, an Indian might take his name. Or others might give him a name. Do you want an Indian name?" asked Many Roads.

Jesse was silent. This was not something he had considered. But "Yes," he said. "That would be an honor."

"I will name you 'Lion Catcher'," said Many Roads. Their eyes met again and they laughed heartily.

It was dark by now, and a large fire was going near the center of the village. Two Indian maids approached with an invitation from the chief to join him for dinner. The boys rose and followed their guides.

They were led through the maze of huts, with the smells of wood smoke and roasting meats in the air, the laughter of children, the barking of dogs. Finally there was Chief Pumpkin Eater, sitting in a large circle, a dozen feet across, with a fire in the center. Seated on the ground in the circle with the chief were the old men of the tribe, with faces darkened and wrinkled by the sun and the wind and the years. A long stemmed pipe was being passed around the circle. To the Chief's immediate left were two empty spaces, for Many Roads and Jesse. The chief gestured and the boys took their places.

Nearby there was a bonfire. There was a large drum surrounded by four drummers, who applied a slow steady beat to the drum. Seated near the drummers was a wrinkled old man shaking a rattle. Flutes and piccolos could be heard from a dozen locations. There were only a few dancers, slowly circling the fire. But it was early. Green palm leaves were lined up on the ground in front of the chief and the elders and Many Roads and Jesse. Baskets and earthenware bowls loaded with assortments of foods were placed on the leaves. "All the food is very good," encouraged Many Roads. "Eat well!"

As the evening progressed, food bowls were emptied and refilled, more dancers joined a growing circle slowly making its way around and around the fire. Jesse noticed that Chief Pumpkin Eater was also wearing one of Many Roads' cougar claws around his neck. Many Roads prophecy was fulfilled. The food was great! And Jesse ate well. Not only was there the venison and turkey that Many Roads had brought, but many other meat, fish and vegetable dishes, with big bowls of corn dumplings and thick corn tortillas, and fragrant melons of every shape, size and color! And bowls of dried dates and berries.

"I must visit my friend often, Chief Pumpkin Eater of the Mojave people, who knows how to live well!" said Many Roads.

"You will always be a welcome sight to these old eyes," replied the chief.

This feast reminded Jesse of nothing he had ever experienced. The closest thing in his memory would be Thanksgiving dinner, when the whole extended family gets together to pig out and toss the Frisbee around. But this was like the whole town having Thanksgiving dinner together, and singing and dancing and tossing the Frisbee around. It was the same spirit in the air, family togetherness and good fellowship. But it was a new and special experience to see the whole town dining and celebrating together, like one big happy family. And from what he had learned, they did not do this just once a year. They didn't need much excuse for these celebrations!

With bellies distended and appetites somewhat abated, conversations sprang up, stories were told. Many Roads brought out his newly made knife to show the chief. The knife was passed around the circle of elders and was admired by all present. The chief was clearly pleased with the finished product and the use to which his antler handle had been put.

Then Many Roads told the chief about the Yuma Indians who had surprised them the previous night. The old chief's face became grave and he sat silently for some time. Then he spoke with great sadness in his voice: "The Yumas west of us have become a problem for me. I cannot find a solution. They steal children from us, and demand ransoms to be paid for the return of the children. If we do not pay, they keep the children as slaves. The ransoms they ask are small, but there is no end to the supply of children for them to steal. And our resources are not great. My people will not feel protected if I let the Yumas keep stealing our children. And they will not be happy if I continue to capitulate and give up our goods for ransoms. But I cannot see a good solution. We are peaceful people, with no history of warfare. The Yumas know this. The Apaches do not attack Mojaves, because there is no pride or glory in it. The Yumas are terrified of the Apaches. In fact, they have the reputation of being cowards, afraid of everyone but the Mojaves. So we peaceful Mojaves have become the perfect prey for them."

"How far is the Yuma village?" asked Many Roads.

"About twenty miles south, on the west side of the river, hidden in a shallow basin" replied the chief.

"How many Mojave children do they hold?" asked Many Roads.

"They recently stole two children, a boy and a girl, 8 and 9 years old. They want two horses for the girl, three for the boy. They are waiting for my answer," said the chief. "They know I will pay. The children will be returned. Then in a few weeks time they will steal more children and demand more ransom."

"How many Yumas are there?" asked Many Roads.

"Maybe two hundred, in that village," replied the chief. "Maybe forty men."

"How many horses do they have?" asked Many Roads.

"I am not sure," replied the chief. "I think they also steal horses, and get them in other ways, to sell or trade. I think the numbers change. They are not known as savvy horse people. It is hard to know how many at any given time."

"Do you have young men here who speak Spanish?" asked Many Roads?

Yes," replied the chief.

"Some of your people are skilled at handling horses?" asked Many Roads

"Yes," answered the chief.

Many Roads was silent and thoughtful. Then "Do you know if the Yuma chief is behind this, or perhaps a young warrior showing off his power?"

"I have given much thought to this question," responded the chief. "You are wise beyond your years, my young friend. I have met their chief. He is old. I think he would seek to avoid trouble with others, at this time in his life. It is my guess that his son, Black Cloud, seeks to advance himself. I send out scouts, to gather information and keep myself informed. I believe Black Cloud is watching the waterholes for a hundred miles or more west of the river, killing and robbing travelers. I know he steals children from other Mojave villages to ransom for horses. I believe he will soon be demanding more than a few horses from the Mojaves."

"What of the Apaches?" asked Many Roads. "Do they know of Black Cloud's ways? Does he have an alliance with them?"

"Again you ask the wisest of questions," responded the chief. "I do not believe the Apaches have been so far west in a long time. They have not troubled the Mojaves. My scouts do not report seeing any Apache sign. I do not think they know of Black Cloud and his ways."

Many Roads and the chief sat in silence for some time.

"What is on your mind, my young friend?" asked the chief.

"Nothing at present," answered Many Roads. "Though things can change. Please, forgive my curiosity and my questions into your affairs. If I think of something helpful, I will share it with you.

I'm truly saddened to learn of your situation. With your permission, I will take a walk by your horse pens and along the river to enjoy this fine evening. Will you join me?"

Jesse, Many Roads and Chief Pumpkin Eater rose and left the others. "The horse pens are this way," motioned the chief. "We let the horses wander free in the daytime, with our young men to watch them. We bring them in at night, to guard against thieves and predators."

"How many do you have?" asked Many Roads.

"Nine," answered the chief, as they approached the brush corral. "We had six times that number before the Yumas began the kidnappings."

"Chief, do you have the clothing or other possessions of Apaches here?" asked Many Roads.

"What do you have in mind, my young friend?" returned the chief.

"I would like a closer look at the Yuma village," answered Many Roads. "If I go as an Apache, and if I am seen, or if the sign I leave is seen, it will make them uneasy. They will think Apaches are watching them. And it will not reveal any interest from the Mojaves."

"Your wisdom is unsettling, in one so young," said the chief. "You will make a great leader for your people one day. Come, let's see what we can find." The chief led them to a hut where they found a group of women eating and resting from the work of cooking. The chief spoke to one of the women, who rose and led the chief and the boys to a long arbor of sticks and poles, with a thatch roof and no walls. There was a sandy floor and nothing else present. The woman pointed at the ground. "Here," she said.

"Dig there," said the chief.

The boys dug with their hands. The sand was loose and moved easily. Six inches below the surface, they found the top of a large wicker basket. More digging revealed a large earthenware jar, covered with a wicker lid, containing many articles of Apache clothing and gear. Knee high leather moccasins, cloth headbands and bandanas, loincloths, leather vests, a bundle of bows and arrows. There was even an Apache medicine man's headdress and deerskin shirt. "Horses?" asked Many Roads.

"Take the things you need from this store and leave the rest here," instructed the chief. "Raven Woman will store it away when you have gone. When you are ready, she will meet you by the horse pens. She will have horses ready with Mexican saddles, food and water. How long will you be gone?"

"Maybe two days," answered Many Roads.

"I will welcome your return." The chief turned and disappeared into the night. Many Roads stooped and selected articles of clothing. He tossed a pair of knee high leather moccasins to Jesse. "See if those fit," he instructed. While Jesse tried on the Apache moccasins, Many Roads put on the Apache clothing. When Jesse looked up the transformation was startling. Many Roads was gone and there stood a wild Apache, right out of the movies. He had unbraided his hair, which was now hanging long and held by a cloth bandana. He wore a knee length fabric loincloth, knee high leather moccasins, and a leather vest. Over his shoulder was his quiver, full of Apache arrows. In his hands were a few items he was offering to Jesse. There was a cotton fabric loincloth, a soft deerskin medicine shirt, and a leather skull cap with six eagle and hawk feathers attached to the crown.

"How do the moccasins fit?" asked Many Roads.

"Fine," answered Jesse. "Do you seriously think I can pass for an Apache?"

"You will be an Apache medicine man," explained Many Roads. "Wear the cap and shirt. I want us to show ourselves to the Yumas, but only from a distance. I want them to think the Apaches are watching them. So, from a distance they will not see a lost white boy, they will only see an Apache warrior with an Apache medicine man. The cowards will keep their distance." Many Roads then turned and walked away into the night. Jesse quickly changed and followed, wearing the Apache moccasins, loincloth, medicine shirt and medicine cap. They met Raven Woman by the horse pens. She had the horses ready to go. Many Roads asked "Can you bring a lariat?"

"Wait," she said. She left and returned quickly, with a coiled Mexican rope, which Many Roads hung on his saddle.

"You can ride a horse?" asked Many Roads.

"I can ride a normal horse," replied Jesse. These horses had leather saddles, stolen by the Apaches from the Mexicans. Each had a leather Mexican water flask and a food bag hanging from the pommel. They looked little different from horses he had ridden before.

"I asked Raven Woman to pick an old quiet horse for you," said Many Roads. "If he gives you any trouble, it is not out of character for an Apache medicine man to walk."

Chapter Ten

As the boys prepared to mount the horses Many Roads warned, "There is danger. You could be injured or killed."

"So could you," replied Jesse.

"Why do you come?" asked Many Roads.

"Without me, you would have no one to catch the lions you shoot." They laughed. "Why do you go?" asked Jesse.

"It is the way home," replied Many Roads. "Do you have your knife?" he asked.

"Yes," replied Jesse.

They mounted their horses.

"Let's take a walk along the river. We'll have some moonlight soon," said Many Roads. He walked his horse from the horse pens to the river, where he turned north along the beach. "We will circle the Mojave village to the north, then travel east for a few miles, then south until we find the Zuni road. We follow that west, back to the river and across. This will put us on the old Mojave road that crosses the gray desert. Then we turn south and follow the river to the Yuma village. If they backtrack us, and they see that our tracks came openly from Apache country, beyond Mojave lands, it will make them believe we are true Apaches. We will return the same way. It is unlikely their scouts will backtrack very far beyond the river. They have not the courage to track Apaches."

Riding a horse through the desert was very different from traveling on foot. Yesterday, he was a lost white boy on foot in the wilderness. Tonight, he is an Apache medicine man on horseback, riding free in his own lands. Somehow, a peak experience occurred, maybe it was the medicine shirt and cap. Lightening flashed in a cloudless sky, and Jesse was channeling the spirit of the wild Apache, steward of the mountains and desert. He grew in his saddle until his head reached the sky. His vision expanded until he could look down and see the Grand Canyon and all the mountains, deserts and prairies beyond spread out at his feet. The sense of freedom that filled his breast was overwhelming, almost too much to contain. He became dizzy and almost fell from his horse. His horse had come to a standstill. When he regained composure, Many Roads had stopped alongside him. Sensing Jesse's experience, he said "It is special, to live free and wild with no fences."

As they rode east the moon rose in the distance. After traveling east several miles, Many Roads turned south. The rising moon was casting long shadows, silhouettes of two Apaches on horseback slipping silently across the sand in the desert night. After about a mile they found the Zuni road and turned west. Soon they reached the river. "It may be shallow enough here for the horses to walk across," advised Many Roads. Indeed, halfway across the ford the horses were no more than belly deep.

They rode west from the river into the moonlit night, their long shadows preceding them. Beyond the greenbelt, about a mile from the river, they turned south and rode through the open desert, their shadows gliding noiselessly over the sand. When the moon was high in the sky and their shadows hid beneath the bellies of the horses, Many Roads stopped. "The Yuma village will be nearby," he said. "We are close. Stay alert, tell me if you hear or smell anything. Remember, you are an Apache, proud and arrogant. Sit tall on your horse." He nudged his horse forward, to walk slowly across the sands. Suddenly they found themselves on the rim of a shallow circular basin, and below them, hidden in the basin, the Yuma village. From their position they could see the river not far beyond the eastern edge of the village, opposite from where they stood. The village was arranged in a circular fashion, with all the huts facing inward. At the center of the village was a large open space, for dancing and meetings and gatherings.

The sleeping village was quiet, brightly lit beneath the high moon. The smoke from several smoldering fires drifted skyward. Suddenly a rider burst into the quiet pre-dawn village from the north, the direction of the Mojave road, from which they had come. He rode straight to one of the huts at the center of the village and dismounted at a run. A figure emerged from the hut and the two engaged in conversation.

"We've been discovered," said Many Roads. "I must take action. If I do not return, go as fast as you can back to the Mojave village. Tell the chief what happened here. Also, tell him the medicine man is responsible for the trouble. He seems to be the head man. Wait here. I will return for you if I am able." With that he nudged his horse into a walk. He walked straight into the village, and suddenly, as he approached the center of the village, he whipped his horse into a wild gallop, straight at the two standing figures. An Apache war cry shattered the still night and chilled the blood of all who heard. Many Roads bore down on the two figures and as he drew close sent an arrow from his bow through the throat of the medicine man. He flew past the medicine man's terrified companion and disappeared into the night beyond the village before the sound of the Apache war cry had faded.

Jesse suddenly felt very much alone, and visible. He wondered what he should do. Many Roads had said he would return. But he didn't say how long to wait here. And he also said to hurry back to the Mojave village and report to Chief Pumpkin Eater. As he sat fidgeting uneasily, "What do you think, Lion Catcher?" asked Many Roads. Jesse was startled and almost fell off his horse. "Good night's work? I think our timing was good and this problem of the Mojave's will be easy to solve."

"Would you not sneak up on me like that?" asked Jesse.

Many Roads chuckled. "Look," he pointed. The village had come alive, like an ant hill someone had stirred with a stick. A group was gathered around the fallen medicine man. Others hustled and bustled around the village. Fires sprang up here and there. Voices could now be heard. "Would you like some more excitement tonight, Lion Catcher?" asked Many Roads. "Or shall we go back and bring the Mojaves?"

"What's on your mind?" answered Jesse.

"If we act now, the Yumas are scared," said Many Roads. "We can take advantage of their fear. It would be easy to take the horses with us. And maybe I can kill Black Cloud. I can see him. I know which one he is. If we could accomplish these things, the Yumas would believe this was an Apache raid and that they have been warned. It would be a long time before the rest of these Yumas would rob and kill travelers at water holes or steal any Mojave children. But if we wait until we return to the Mojave village and consult with Chief Pumpkin Eater, who knows what we will find on returning here? Or how events might develop. They might kill the children, or move the village, and the horses. I feel it is the right choice to act now."

"I haven't caught any lions yet tonight," replied Jesse.

"Come," said Many Roads. He started his horse at a walk, circling the village toward the horse pens. As they walked he instructed Jesse: "I will give you the lariat, with the loop around the neck of a single horse. Lead him north, to the Mojave road, and return to the Mojave village. Every herd of horses has a leader. If you lead the leader, the other horses will follow. I will come behind to drive them and herd the stragglers. You go at a walk. I do not expect the Yumas to follow. If anyone troubles us, I will take action. You continue."

At the horse corrals they stopped to survey the animals. "More than one hundred horses," observed Many Roads. "Good. Chief Pumpkin Eater will be pleased." He slipped from his saddle, lariat in hand, and entered the brush corral. He slipped the loop over the head of the horse he judged to be leader and returned to Jesse with the rope, but left the brush corral closed. "Wait for my return," he said. He mounted his horse and began walking slowly toward the center of the village.

As Jesse watched, Many Roads walked his horse among the huts, meandering to a position giving him a good view of the figures in the center of the village. He sent an arrow among them. There was a scream, and Jesse had no doubt that the arrow had taken the life of Black Cloud. The rest of the figures scattered. Immediately the entire village was screaming in terror and running in panic. Jesse heard the name of 'Geronimo' being screamed into the night.

Many Roads rode silently into the center of the panicked village. He rode up to a pair of children standing alone, stopped a moment, then turned and rode to the corral with the children trotting behind him on foot. When they arrived at the corral, Many Roads addressed the children: "I am a friend of Chief Pumpkin Eater. I have come to take you home. Do you know how to ride a horse?"

"Yes," replied the boy.

"Yes," replied the girl.

"Good," said Many Roads. He found many bridles hanging on a bush, selected two, and entered the brush corral. He put the bridles on two of the horses, boosted each child up onto one of the horses. "Just ride quietly. Each of you ride your horse on opposite sides of the herd. If any horse tries to leave, chase him back in. Remain silent. We will be at your village in the morning. If there is trouble, run into the desert and hide. Bury yourself in the sand. When it is safe, go east, into the rising sun, as far as the river. There you will see your village."

"Look out," called Jesse. "A Yuma!" He pointed. A Yuma youth approaching the horses had seen them and was calling out. Many Roads drew his bow and pointed an arrow at the youth but did not shoot.

The youth turned and ran screaming in fear, "Geronimo! Geronimo!" No one else would come near the horse pens this night.

Many Roads opened up the brush corral and pointed north. Jesse led off as he had been instructed. The two children rode as instructed. Many Roads quietly herded the horses and followed behind.

Mojave Desert Oasis with Date Palms

Chapter Eleven

The ride back to the Mojave village in the dawn light was spectacular though uneventful. The Yumas did not follow, and there was no trouble. When the group reached the river, Many Roads called out to Jesse, "Continue east on the Zuni road. Follow the same path we used last night." Jesse led the horses in a wide circle, east and north, around the Mojave village and returned to the horse pens. Many Roads approached the children. "Go find Chief Pumpkin Eater. Ask him to send some boys to help with the horses." The children jumped from their horses and left at a run.

Very soon the old chief arrived, amazed at the sight of the horses. When he heard their account of happenings at the Yuma village, he was even more amazed. "This problem has been troubling me for many months. Yet, you have come along and solved it in a night. The Mojaves are in your debt."

Many Roads said "There is no debt. Give me three of the horses to continue on my way. They will take us across the gray desert in comfort, and they will make a fine gift for my people at Mono Lake." The old chief was eager to comply. "Take the herd, if you like. It rightfully belongs to you. I did not take it from the Yumas."

"Three horses. We will eat and sleep here tonight and leave tomorrow," he announced.

"I will be sad to see you depart," said the old chief. "Please come see me when you can. I will always be happy to see you."

"Thank you," said Many Roads. "But I am on a mission to show this white boy the way home. We will continue tomorrow."

The boys slept most of the day. When they woke in the afternoon they found another feast being prepared. After a swim in the river, they ate well that evening and slept that night in the hut in the Mojave village. The next morning, they dressed in their own clothing, and Many Roads braided his hair again. They left the Apache clothing on their beds. A squaw brought them breakfast of smoked fish, hot pumpkin stew with corn dumplings, sliced melon, and dried dates. When they were finished, Chief Pumpkin Eater arrived to walk with them to the horse pens. "I sent scouts to the Yuma village while you slept," said the chief. "They have just now returned. They found the village empty. All the Yumas have fled. Many of their belongings are still in the huts. Food is still in the baskets, fires still smoldering. But no Yumas. There will be no more trouble from them."

As they approached the horse pens, The chief pointed, "There are three horses, with two Mexican saddles and a pack frame, and burden baskets full of good things to eat. There's a big pumpkin tied up on top of the pack frame for your family at Mono Lake. The mother of the children you brought home put a bag of dried dates in the basket to thank you. Your tanned furs are tied on the pack frame, and the tanned deer skin, as well."

"Thank you," said Many Roads, "for your friendship and your hospitality. You have become like a beloved uncle to me. Take care of yourself until we meet again."

"It tears my heart to see you go," said the chief. "I pray you have safe and happy trails, Many Roads."

The boys led their horses to the river bank and turned south toward the Zuni road and the ford. They walked the mile to the ford, where they mounted and crossed the river. As they took to the Mojave Road, Many roads said "I do not think any Yumas will be threatening this road or the waterholes today. So we will travel openly. If we encounter any Yumas I will face them. The first waterhole beyond the river is fifty miles west."

They traveled through desert that was now gray, with no longer any sign of the red or pink color. They were still in the Joshua tree forest. With the rising sun at their backs, and their shadows long before them, the boys rode into the gray desert dawn. Jesse could not avoid the thought that came to him: Even with a 4-wheel drive convoy and all the gear and supplies available to modern travelers, crossing this desert with fifty miles between water holes is a trip that only the boldest would attempt. Yet, he was quite comfortable here, on foot or horseback, and had no wish to hurry the experience or to be anywhere else. He was no longer the same lost person who had set out from the Grand Canyon two weeks ago.

At midday they stopped for food. They sat on the ground in the shade of their horses and split one of the melons the Mojave women had put in their baskets. There were also some dried dates, sugar sweet, and cold corn tortillas. After lunch they mounted and continued their trek toward the first waterhole. The terrain here was flat gray desert, sand and shale, with ridges of those ragged, jagged broken tooth mountains rising from the plain here and there in the distance. The flora was

Joshua trees, some sparse low growing sage, and one small stunted kind of prickly pear. These were growing fewer and farther between as they advanced. The landscape was growing increasingly harsh and barren with each passing mile.

As evening approached they had come more than forty miles from the river. Suddenly, the road dipped down to cross an arroyo. They were surprised by a rocky pool of water, spring fed and surrounded by vegetation. This was the first water they had seen in this dry land since leaving the river almost fifty miles behind.

"Is this one of the water holes where the Yumas were robbing and killing travelers?" asked Jesse.

Many Roads nodded. "If you travel through this country you must come here. It is the only water in this land. Pumas, jaguars, coyotes and rattlesnakes know this and come here to hunt. The Yumas know this and would camp here, waiting for the weary and thirsty traveler to arrive. They would kill him, take everything he has and leave his body for the coyotes and vultures. If you scout the area, you will find human bones. But no more. For a time this road and the water holes are safe from the treacherous Yumas."

The boys filled their water flasks, drank, splashed themselves, let the horses drink. They made a cold dinner on things from their food baskets and camped in the arroyo by the road that night. The next morning they were up at first light, had a melon for breakfast, mounted their horses and took to the road again, to ride in the cool dawn air.

Paiute House and Baskets with Cinder Cones in the Distance

Many Roads left the Mojave Road and turned northwest from the water hole. "We will have a long ride today," he said. "No more water for another fifty miles. Tonight we camp at a place with pools of hot water. It is near a Paiute village. Chief Tecopa will welcome us, and we will sleep beside his hot water pools."

All day they marched through the empty gray desert, stopping for a lunch of melon. In the afternoon, Jesse noticed that the land had become increasingly empty of most vegetation. The desert was flat, gray sand and shale, and had taken on an otherworldly, surreal quality. In the distance ahead of them were low hills of sand and beyond those were volcanic cinder cones and ridges of bleak treeless mountains. As evening approached, they arrived at the hot water pools. Here too the land was flat and bare, with little vegetation other than the tall coarse grass that grew along the edges of the hot water pools. Jesse could see several small pools, or ponds, crystal clear and shallow, with smooth muddy bottoms and no plant life.

Many Roads picked a suitable spot near the water's edge and got down from his horse. After unloading the horses, they dined on food from their baskets, then fell asleep on the ground by the water, exhausted from their long day's ride. After it was full dark, Jesse woke under a desert moon to find Many Roads gone. He sat alone on the shore looking up at the stars. Then he realized that Many Roads' loincloth and weapons were on the ground where he had been sleeping. Jesse looked over the water and saw Many Roads in the middle of the pool. He removed his sandals and stepped into the water. It was hot, and the bottom soft and muddy, squishing between his toes. It felt good. He quickly shucked his clothing and joined Many

Roads. The water was hot, like being in a steam bath. He was quickly sweating. He turned on his back to float in the heated pool in the desert night looking out at the milky way and the seemingly endless reach of stars.

Chapter Twelve

The next morning the boys woke by the edge of the hot water pool. "What is this place?" asked Jesse.

"These pools of hot water are on the lands of the Paiute people," answered Many Roads. "Tecopa is their chief. Yet, all other Indian tribes are free to come here to soak in the pools. Some come in winter for relief from the cold. Old people come because the waters have power to heal the pains of old age. Sick people come to the waters for healing. Indian people have always come here, as far back as our stories and legends go. No one knows how long people have been coming here. Chief Tecopa makes all people welcome. All who come here put aside grievances. There are no robbings or killings, not even quarrels. This is a special place. And all the tribes respect it."

"Someone comes," said Jesse, pointing.

Many Roads turned to look. "Chief Tecopa," he said.

The boys rose from the ground as the chief approached. "I was told you were here, Many Roads," said the chief. "Why did you not come to the village?" he asked.

"We arrived at sundown, very tired," answered Many Roads. "We came fifty miles through the heart of the gray desert. After a soak in the pools, I could not go further than the shore. We slept right here and have just awakened. But we will join you now for some food."

"Come," invited Chief Tecopa.

As they approached the village in company with Chief Tecopa, Jesse noticed that the village differed in appearance from the Chemahuevi, Mojave or Yuma villages. These houses were round instead of square or rectangle. They were made of sticks for a framework, and thatched with grass and reeds, like the other desert dwellings. But each had only a door opening instead of the whole front being open. And most striking, all the huts faced east, in the same direction.

After a morning meal of mesquite beans with Chief Tecopa, it transpired that the village was low on meat, and some of the boys of the tribe were preparing for a turkey hunt that day. Many Roads volunteered to join them. Many Roads and Jesse left the pack horse and all their belongings in the village and rode their horses out behind the group of six boys, each armed with a stout striking stick, about three feet long. One of the boys, Hawk, who seemed to know and admire Many Roads, walked alongside his horse. "Yesterday," he said, "I saw a flock of a hundred turkeys, not far. Turkeys are rare in our territory. These were in some brush near the base of those hills straight ahead."

As they walked, Many Roads asked "Do you have a plan for hunting the turkeys?"

"We don't often get a chance to hunt them," Hawk replied. "But we have had success by driving the flock slowly until they begin to tire. When they tire, they drop down on the ground and try to hide and avoid us. Then we rush among them and kill them with sticks."

"That sounds like an excellent plan," said Many Roads. "I have hunted turkeys that way with good results. Lion Catcher and I will hold back, until the birds begin to tire. When you rush them, some will take to the air. We will ride our horses beneath them and kill them with sticks. See if you can find us some striking sticks before we get there."

As they rode Many Roads spoke to Jesse. "Hawk will find us some striking sticks. We will follow the boys as they spread out and drive the turkeys. When they rush the turkeys, some will try to fly away from pursuit. We will ride our horses beneath them and kill them with the sticks. Strike for their long neck. If you hit the neck or head it will bring them down."

As they approached the hills they entered a zone of grass and low brush. The boys spread out to locate the flock of turkeys. Many Roads and Jesse stood their horses and waited. Soon one of the boys called out and the others converged on him. As they approached his location, Jesse began to hear the sounds of the turkeys' nervous gobbling. He and Many Roads followed slowly on the horses. The boys made a line as they moved through the brush, herding and driving the turkeys into a group, moving them forward. After they had moved about a quarter mile through the grass and brush, as expected, the turkeys began to tire. They started dropping to the ground and trying to hide. Then the boys broke into a run and rushed into the flock of turkeys, swinging their sticks and calling out to frighten and confuse the birds. As the boys began to strike and kill turkeys, some of them took flight. Then Many Roads and Jesse kicked their horses into motion and rode beneath the flying turkeys, swinging their sticks and bringing down the clumsy birds. This was the first time Jesse had ever ridden a horse so wildly and with such abandon. It was the first time he had hunted. His blood grew hot with the excitement. And he joined in the hunt with enthusiasm. After the boys could find no more turkeys to swing their sticks at, they began to scour the brush and gather the turkeys they had killed. They piled them and counted nineteen turkeys. They also found one antelope that Many roads had shot with his bow.

The hunting party was fortunate to have Many Roads and Jesse along with their horses. The boys found some hemp plants and made cord to tie the turkey legs together. They hung all the turkeys on the two horses, and draped the antelope over the saddle of one. Many Roads and Jesse walked back to the village with the boys, leading the game laden horses.

It was a successful hunt. By the time they returned to the village, most of the day was gone. Chief Tecopa and the villagers were happy to see so many turkeys, and an antelope! Since the village seemed to be suffering a shortage of food, Many Roads contributed the huge pumpkin given them by Chief Pumpkin Eater, and the few melons they had left in their food baskets. As they dined on turkey and pumpkin and antelope that evening, Many Roads related the story of the Mojaves and Yumas, and of how he and Jesse had fooled the Yumas and discouraged them from robbing, killing and kidnapping. The Paiutes listened with rapt attention, young and old alike, hanging on his every word. Everyone loves a story.

They slept in the Paiute village that night. Next morning, after a cold breakfast, Chief Tecopa announced that a gathering party was going to a hidden oasis to gather dates from the palm trees. Jesse loved dates. And their supply was dwindling.

Mojave Date Palms

So the boys decided to join the work party. The group set out in a northwesterly direction, across the flat desert terrain, toward a line of ragged black mountains in the distance. As they rode behind the children and squaws, Many Roads offered insight. "Though this terrain looks bleak and barren," he said, "when you are close to the hills and mountains, you find many ravines, clefts and canyons. Hidden in some of these are oases, with cool streams and pools, little waterfalls, vegetation and palm trees, game to hunt, very beautiful and happy places to rest. I am not here to help with the work, but to soak in a cool pool, to rest, and to replenish our supply of dates."

After filling their baskets with dates, they spent the day in the cool water, or lounging by the water, while the Paiute women and children gathered dates. In the late afternoon, Many roads left the group and returned in an hour with seven rabbits which he gave to one of the squaws. The women made a fire and prepared a meal of rabbit, mesquite beans and dried dates. After listening to stories by Many Roads, they all slept on the ground beside a large pool. Next morning the group returned to the village, with all the burden baskets full of dates.

That evening they dined on turkey and antelope and licorice flavored mesquite beans. Again, Many Roads told stories about his adventures. The Paiutes enjoyed his stories and begged for more, even when he announced that he was tired and ready for sleep.

The next morning, after a breakfast of mesquite beans, Many Roads and Jesse loaded the horses and said farewell to Chief Tecopa, thanking him for his hospitality. They set out to the northwest, following the same path to the oasis where they had gathered dates. Today, they entered the canyon where the oasis was located, passed through the oasis and beyond, out the other end of the canyon.

As they left the narrow canyon they entered a landscape like nothing Jesse had ever seen. They were in the bottom of a wide, deep valley (Death Valley), near the southeast corner. The scale of size and distances overwhelmed the senses. The bottom of the valley was flat as a table, like an ancient lake or seabed, with not a blade of grass or any sort of vegetation to be seen. The valley was ten miles or more wide and its length ran out of sight to the north. The western wall of the valley was an imposing range of ragged black mountains, almost three miles high! On the east side of the valley another range of mountains, only a mile high, with many shapes, soft contours, clefts and rivulets sculpted and smoothed by wind and water over eons of time. The colors of the mountains on the eastern side of the valley were more interesting than the forbidding black mountains on the west, with bands of color in soft muted shades of gray and gold, copper, red, pink, orange, bronze green, yellow, ivory. Yet there was no sign of water or trees or plant life anywhere. The land appeared completely bare and devoid of life. Not a blade of grass was to be seen.

"This desert valley is Shoshone country," said Many Roads. "They are not very friendly to others than themselves. But since my tribe occupies lands to the north and south and west of them, I have come to know many of them. We can pass through here in safety. Though the lack of food, water and shelter make this valley a hot and dangerous place to travel. There is a large oasis about twenty miles north, on the valley floor, with hot water pools, cool water, and date palms. We will camp there tonight. As we go we can find cool streams and oases in the canyons of the hills to the east."

The scale of this valley was so vast that after walking for hours it did not seem like they had advanced at all. They finally arrived at the oasis in the evening, made camp by a pool of cool water, in the shade of a stand of date palms. "I have never seen any place like this desolate valley," said Many Roads. "It has a strange atmosphere, a deadly kind of beauty. I like to pass through here."

Jesse became aware that there were Indians camped at the oasis. He nudged Many Roads and pointed. "They are Shoshones," said Many Roads. "This valley is their territory. But just over these black mountains to the west is the land of my people. These Shoshones know me and will not trouble us. Tribes in this area, and in the mountains where I live, are not like the Yumas. Some Shoshones can be troublesome. But people north of Yuma country generally live in peace, without troubling or killing one another. These Shoshones will ignore us."

The Sand Dunes

Chapter Thirteen

Next morning after breakfast, the boys set out to the north, staying close to the east side of the valley. After leaving the oasis, the flat, firm valley floor soon became rolling sand dunes, that grew higher with each passing mile. The valley grew steadily wider. By afternoon the valley was twenty miles or more wide and the heat was intense. Mirages shimmered and danced everywhere, playing tricks on the eye and the mind.

Many Roads turned into a side canyon and shortly they were in another grotto oasis, with date palms and shade and pools of cool water. "We will rest here, tonight and tomorrow," said Many Roads. "We will leave here just before dark tomorrow and travel across the sand dunes at night. We should be across them and at the base of the mountains to the west by daybreak. It is hotter in the dunes than here along the edge of the valley. And hard walking for the horses. There is no water until we get into the canyons on the other side. Even at night it is hot in the dunes."

The boys stripped and got into one of the cool pools to soak and refresh themselves. The horses drank. Later Many Roads found rabbits, which they had with dates for their dinner. They alternately slept and soaked and ate, all night and all of the following day. In the evening, after the sun dipped behind the peaks of the western mountains, but with dusk still lingering, they set out directly west through the heart of the sand dunes. There was not a blade of grass or a plant of any kind. Just twenty endless miles of rolling dunes to be crossed. Daylight went and night descended. The eye could not see but the horses knew where the other side was. And they plodded steadily through the darkness. Late in the night half a moon rose behind them. With its light reflected off the dunes, the night was suddenly bright as a silver day. And the horses plodded steadily on. Jesse felt like they were moving in a dream, ceaselessly walking but going nowhere. He realized the heat and the hypnotic rhythm of the plodding horse were affecting his mind. "I'll have to watch that," he thought. "Watch what?" he responded. As the dusky pre-dawn light displaced the night, Jesse noticed that the dunes were growing lower, then firmer. Soon the horses' hooves made sounds on the firm ground. The dunes were behind them. "Could we have crossed these dunes without the horses?" he wondered.

As the day dawned, they entered the foothills of the western mountains. Many Roads found a canyon that he seemed to be looking for. They wandered through barren black volcanic rock canyons, empty and devoid of plant life or water. About midday, they entered a small valley, where vegetation began to appear, small prickly pear cactus and thin tufts of grass, and there was a stream. They stopped here for rest and food, and to refresh themselves in the cool water. Then after a nap they decided to stay there and rest for the balance of the day and to sleep there that night.

The next day they continued to wander through the canyons and valleys. They wandered for a week, in and out of canyon and valley, some bare and some with water and vegetation. They moved slowly higher in the terrain. "These mountains are like a maze," said Many Roads. "They are wide and wander endlessly. Sometimes the canyons lead in circles or come to blind ends. But I have been through here, one time with a friend who knows these mountains well. I know the way through the canyons, and I like to travel here. It is an unusual place."

Jesse was glad to learn that Many Roads was confident of the way. After a week of wandering through the mountain canyons and valleys, they struck a trail that climbed along the wall on one side of a narrow valley. The trail was only a foot wide in places, and the drop so long that Jesse had to turn his face away in fear and hope the horse had a strong sense of self-preservation.

They crossed through a high mountain pass. Then the trail descended for a time, then climbed again, twisting and turning. As they went higher, and farther north, the rock of the mountains changed from the rough black volcanic rock to rusty orange, and then to smooth white stone. The black volcanic landscape had been scattered with small stunted prickly pear cactus and not much else. In the rusty orange zone there were stands of pinion pine and cactus. In the smooth white mountains there was an occasional gnarled and twisted pine tree (bristlecone pine), of a kind Jesse had never seen, and an occasional alpine flower. They had short, thick trunks, twenty to thirty feet tall and four feet thick or more. As they climbed, more of these trees dotted the bare white stony peaks, springing right out of the white stone, out of cracks and clefts in the rock, clinging perilously to the edges of the cliffs. The trees grew larger and more numerous as they went higher. They appeared to be ancient. Most of them seemed as if they had survived repeated blasting by lightening and storm.

Then suddenly as they crested a rise, a scene spread out before them that made Jesse gasp with astonishment. Ten thousand feet below spread a great desert valley (Owens Valley), ten miles wide, that ran to north and south as far as the eye could see. On the other side of this valley was a beautiful ten-thousand foot high snow-capped gray granite mountain range. By simply turning your head to north and south you could see the entire 500 mile long range! There was haze on the valley floor. And the mountain range seemed to float on the haze as though on water. This had to be one of the most spectacular and breathtaking sights Jesse had ever seen.

"My people live in a deep grassy valley high in those mountains," said Many Roads. "Our valley is just about straight across from where we stand. It is the best place on earth to live. There are many waterfalls and streams; a gentle river runs through green meadows; there are oak and pine forests for food, herds with hundreds of deer, many black bears, swarms of fish in the waters. It is the most beautiful place on earth. This is a view of our mountains that I would like to enjoy. The air is cool here. We will camp here and watch the sun go down behind the mountains and resume our journey tomorrow."

Chapter Fourteen

The next day the boys descended from the heights down into the valley. There was a heavily used road traveling north and south along the center of the valley. The boys turned north and after a few miles found a grove of cottonwood trees with a stream where they decided to make an early camp. The next day they struck out north again and covered many miles that day. On the following day, about midday, they crested a low rise in the land and came on a view of Mono Lake and the otherworldly terrain surrounding it. The lake was approximately circular in shape and about ten miles across, with a pointed cinder cone rising out of the exact center of the lake.

Many Roads pointed to a place on the western lakeshore. "There is one of our villages," he said. Jesse could see in the hazy distance a group of desert huts clustered by the edge of the water. The village looked much like the Paiute village where they had stayed with Chief Tecopa and his people. The lake was huge, and glassy smooth. Beyond the far northern shore was a low spur of mountains. The eastern shore could barely be seen. There was sparse vegetation here on the valley floor. In the area immediately surrounding the lake, vegetation was not in evidence at all. The earth was soft and fluffy, the land was colored in soft shades of gold, tan and pink, with spires that stuck straight up out of the ground or out of the water's edge, some of them small as your arm and some as big as tree trunks. The spires gave the landscape an off planet kind of feeling, like being in a scene in a *Starwars* movie.

They headed for the village, and as they drew close Jesse could see that these huts were like those in the Paiute village and all of them were also facing east. As they came near the village youngsters ran out to greet them. When they recognized Many Roads the level of their excitement increased. They stopped the horses at the edge of the village and dismounted. Many Roads untied the bundle of furs and removed it from the pack horse. By now he had more than twenty rabbit skins, the cougar rug and the deerskin. He untied the burden baskets laden with dates and other food. He picked up one burden basket and the furs, gesturing to Jesse to pick up the other basket. Carrying these, he walked into the village to a hut where Jesse saw an old squaw with gray in her long black hair sitting on the earth in front of her hut repairing a burden basket. She was surrounded by ten or more large, conical burden baskets. When she saw Many Roads she smiled and rose to greet him. He walked quietly up to her and offered the bundle of furs. "It is good to see you looking well, Sky Dancer," he said. "Here are some furs to make your house more comfortable. And some dates from the Mojave country."

Sky Dancer accepted the gifts and asked "Are you hungry?"

"We could eat," answered Many Roads.

"Sit and I will feed you," she said. "The house where you stayed when you came through last time is still empty. You may use it again. Or you may sleep on the ground by my fire if you wish." She brought the boys basket bowls of the licorice flavored mesquite beans, two roasted quail, a bowl of manzanita berries, and a small bowl of pine nuts. Many Roads dumped half of the pine nuts into his mesquite beans, and Jesse followed suit by dumping the rest into his own bowl. As the boys ate, Sky Dancer said to Many Roads "You come at a good time. We are gathering winter food. Today we have been gathering the fly larvae from the lake, and tomorrow the whole village will climb into the mountains where there is a pine forest with a good crop of pine cones ready to harvest. Two strong young men might be very helpful." She smiled broadly.

"You know that I always enjoy the pine nut harvest," said Many Roads. "I am happy that we have come at this time. Where is the fly harvest? After our food is finished, we can help with that."

"I am going there soon," said she. "You can join me. I was gathering this morning. I came here to eat and repair this basket. We can go when you are ready." She gathered her hair and coiled it atop her head, placing a small basket like a cap on her head to hold the hair in place and out of her way for the afternoon's work. "We have been gathering the fly larvae for ten days," offered Sky Dancer. "Today will be the last."

After the meal, they each picked up two large cone shaped burden baskets and a flat fan shaped basket. They followed Sky Dancer out of the village and along the lake shore to a place where other women and children were working to gather fly larvae. "Mono Lake is the only place where these flies live," offered Many Roads. "The larvae hatch under the water and float to the surface. When they reach the air, the breeze across the lake surface blows them across the surface of the water. If the wind blows them ashore, as it does today, we take the wide flat basket and sweep clouds of the hatchlings into these big burden baskets. When your basket is two-thirds full, give it to one of the squaws. She will give you an empty basket to fill again."

All afternoon the boys worked in the sun along the water's edge with the women, sweeping vast quantities of fly larvae into the baskets. The setting and the stunning off-planet beauty of the surrounding landscape brought a sense of joy to Jesse as he worked. Somewhere other women received the baskets of harvested flies and worked to prepare and store the harvest for use through the winter and throughout the year, until the next harvest the following year.

That evening Chief Fox Shadow returned from a day of hunting. He was happy to see Many Roads, who presented the three horses to the chief as a gift. As they shared the evening meal, the chief told the boys of the pending pine nut harvest. "There is a pine forest up in the mountains," the chief explained. "Each year at this time we move the whole village, and we camp in the pine forest and work together until the harvest is finished. This harvest is important to us. It provides an essential staple food for the whole village, for the whole year. And the surplus is used to trade for other foods from the villages in the mountains. This year we will trade for acorns and dried fish, with the Ahwahneechees. I am happy to see you here for the pine nut harvest, Many Roads. You are a good worker."

The next morning after breakfast the entire village packed up their belongings and made ready for departure. The men and older boys carried rolls of furs for bedding, women carried stacks of burden baskets to collect the pine nuts. The three horses were loaded with food for the tribe. Three of the older boys carried twenty foot long willow poles, for reaching into the trees to knock down pine cones. They set out in single file, heading west for the mountains. There were no foothills to speak of. The flat floor of the desert valley ran right up to the foot of the granite mountains, which seemed to spring right out of the desert sands.

They found a rocky trail and began to climb, into the mouth of a broad, steep gorge, a half mile wide and more than a mile deep, with a crystal clear rushing stream cascading down its center from the high country. They climbed through lush green meadows and stands of alder trees with smooth silver trunks and broad green leaves, the slightest breeze causing them to flash and flicker in the mountain sunshine. The trail climbed above the alders, then narrowed and climbed among scattered pines. It climbed above the pines and up the bare granite face of one of the canyon walls. The trail grew steeper with each mile. The tribe climbed all day. As they got closer to the top, the trail was so steep they were stepping from rock to rock, like climbing a staircase. This was a very difficult trail for horses. But these horses seemed not to notice. Maybe they had been Apache horses and were used to rough going, in the desert mountains of Arizona and Mexico.

By late afternoon they were cresting a high mountain pass, very nearly as high as you can go in these mountains. Jesse judged that they were at ten thousand feet, as high today as they were in the white mountains days ago, looking across the broad valley at these granite mountains. Just beyond the pass was a crystal clear alpine lake (Ellery Lake), half a mile long and a quarter mile wide, surrounded by bare granite peaks dotted with pine trees.

Unlike the sweltering heat on the valley floor, the air up here was cool and refreshing. The tribe found a place on the lake shore to camp for the evening, beneath a stand of pine trees on a bluff thirty feet above the water. Some of the boys gathered fallen limbs and cones from the scattered pine trees for firewood. Other boys slipped silently into the water of the lake below the camp and caught trout by hand. The squaws began preparing food for dinner. The men rolled out the bedding of bearskins or sheepskins for sleeping on the ground beneath the pines, with woven rabbit skin blankets for covers. Jesse had learned from the Indians that to them the great outdoors was like a vast garden they lived in. In this setting on the shore of a crystal lake, high in these granite mountains, beneath a dome of stars, he understood their love of the outdoors and shared it. "There is no place on earth I'd rather be," he thought. "Why would I want to be indoors right now?"

Chapter Fifteen

The next day, after a breakfast of fresh trout and Mesquite beans, the tribe set out. The trail climbed at a gentle rate, and soon passed another alpine lake (Tioga Lake), the same in size as the one lower down where they had camped. The trail wandered among granite peaks, through high alpine meadows a mile or more across, thick with wildflowers, wide open to the sky, with wild streams meandering. All around were majestic snow capped granite peaks thrusting up into a lapis blue sky. The air was cool and fresh. Suddenly the desert was gone and Jesse wondered if he had died and gone to heaven. They skirted a third crystal clear alpine lake (Lake Tenaya), twice the size of the first two. Beyond the lake they entered a forest of towering sweet smelling pines. As they continued, the forest grew thicker for several miles. Then the entire tribe stopped in a wide clearing with a crystal clear stream to drink and fish in. They began to make fires and prepare food. By then it was late in the day.

In the summertime weather the tribe felt no need for erecting shelters. They were happy living and sleeping among the pines beneath the open sky.

Two of the boys were fishing in the stream, with long slender spears they had brought along. Other boys and girls gathered firewood. The men scouted the forest to look for the thickest crop of pine cones for tomorrow's gathering.

Many Roads and Jesse wandered off together. Many Roads seemed to follow a trail that he knew well, which climbed above the forest and up the slope of one of the granite peaks, to the very top, until they were standing on the very summit, gazing over the surrounding mountain terrain. The view before them seemed like a gigantic rock garden composed of granite boulders a mile in diameter. The scale of things up here was disorienting. "There is the valley where my tribe lives," said Many Roads, pointing. Among the granite peaks, Jesse could see a cleft. But he could not really see anything of the valley.

"My tribe has many stories, about these rocks and waters and animals," said Many Roads. "You see that peak over there?" he pointed. "The one that is round on top?"

"I see it," Jesse replied.

"That is the squaw, Tis-sa-ack," spoke Many Roads. "One very warm day, To-ko-ya and his wife, Tis-sa'-ack, were traveling from the high country, where we are now. They had been here wandering and gathering food, and were on their way back down that canyon yonder, into our valley. He carried a heavy roll of bearskins and rabbit fur blankets that was their bed; she carried the burden basket with the supply of pine nuts they had gathered. To-ko'-ya was hot and tired and walked slowly, while Tis-sa'-ack walked ahead of her husband. She reached Mirror Lake, near the mouth of the canyon, well ahead of him and, thirsty, she drank. Her thirst was not easily quenched. She drank and she drank until there was not a drop of water left in Mirror Lake. When To-ko'-ya arrived at the lake, hot and thirsty, there was no water for him to drink. Angry he beat Tis-sa'-ack with his staff; she reviled him and threw her basket at him; they both turned to stone for their shameful behavior.

"There you see Tis-sa'-ack (Half Dome), on the south side of the canyon, turned to stone for arguing with her husband; you can still see her image on the face of the rock.

Across the canyon, on the north side, stands To-ko'-ya (North Dome), turning away from the thrown basket. And to his right the small round rock (Basket Dome) is the basket she threw at him during the argument.

"To beat one's wife or children is the most shameful of behaviors to my people. Or for a wife to argue with her husband. These rocks are here to remind us every day to be kind to one another, to help each other in life."

"We have stories about every rock and stream, every waterfall or animal," said Many Roads.

"Tis-sa'-ack" now named Half Dome

"To-ko'-ya" now named North Dome
Basket Dome is at far right partially hidden

As Jesse looked at the round peak that Many Roads called Tis-sa-ack, he realized that he had seen this rock before, though not from this angle. He believed this was Half Dome in Yosemite Valley. And the name of Mirror Lake was a familiar name. His family had vacationed in Yosemite Valley one summer. "What is the name for your valley?" he asked.

"We call it Deep Grassy Valley," Many Roads responded.

"Is this Yosemite Valley?" Jesse asked.

"Yosemite?" laughed Many Roads. "That sounds like the Paiute word for 'big grizzly bear'," said Many Roads. Sometimes a grizzly bear will enter our valley. They are killers. So we hunt them. We have learned ways to kill grizzly bears. The tribes in the lands west of these mountains began to call our tribe grizzly bears, because we are fierce enough to hunt them. Our chief, Tenaya, is happy to know that. He says that if we have such a fierce reputation, maybe they will not want to come here and disturb our peace and quiet."

Chapter Sixteen

The next day, after a sumptuous breakfast of fresh mountain trout, mesquite beans and fresh berries, the tribe gathered and followed one of the men through the forest. The morning air was heavy with the sweet vanilla scent of the pines. About a quarter mile from camp they stopped and burst into a flurry of activity. Some of the squaws began to remove leaves and sticks from a shallow roasting pit that looked like it had been used many times before. This roasting pit might have been in this pine forest and used by generation after generation of mountain Indians for a thousand years or more. Other squaws and young girls began to gather fallen pine cones into big piles on the forest floor. Boys and girls gathered firewood and piled it by the roasting pit. Men moved among the trees knocking pine cones loose from the tree limbs with the long willow poles. Some of the boys climbed the trees to dislodge pine cones. All kinds of pine cones were fair game: big ones, little ones, fat ones, skinny ones, ripe ones, green ones, they all came down.

As the cones accumulated on the forest floor, the women and girls gathered, sorted and piled them. Then they loaded them into the burden baskets and moved them to bigger piles near the roasting pit. They worked until midday when they stopped for food. Roasting fires were started in the pit the women had cleaned out. As they ate their lunch, they began to pick and eat pine nuts from the ripe brown cones whose petals were beginning to open, one seed at the base of each petal. They ate to their heart's content.

After lunch, when the fires had burned down to a bed of coals, the women and girls began pushing the green unopened cones into the pit to roast in the fire. They watched the cones closely, turning them with sticks. And when one began to open from the heat they would remove it from the pit with a stick. Men and women, boys and girls sat in groups picking pine nuts from the cones, one nut at a time, all afternoon and into the night, until all the cones were opened and picked clean.

They slept there that night. The next morning after breakfast, they repeated the activities of the previous day and evening. When there were no more pine cones to be reached, the tribe moved to a new location in the forest and continued the pine nut harvest. At each location, there was an ancient roasting pit. Clearly, people had been coming to these pine forests to harvest pine cones in this way for a very long time.

Though they labored, there was an attitude of play and frolic, as well. These were happy people, nice people to be with. They stayed in the pine forest many days, until they had gathered all the pine nuts they would need for the year. It was more than the people and all three horses could carry. So they left some behind, with several boys who stayed to protect it from animals. Others would return in a few days to carry the rest of the pine nuts down into Ahwahnee for trading with the Ahwahneechees.

Many Roads and Jesse decided to part company with the Mono people and head down into Ahwahnee. They said their goodbyes near the shore of the upper lake. Then Many Roads led off and found a trail that circled the lake. At the western edge of the lake, the trail turned away from the water and began a slow descent into the canyon that led down into Ahwahnee, now only about ten miles away.

The day was early. Many Roads stopped and seemed to be lost in thought as he stared at one of the nearby peaks. "There is an old hermit who lives in a cave up on that peak," he gestured. "He stays up there all year round. He knows which plants are good for medicine. People from the mountains and desert come here to ask him for healing. They pay him with food. And they send boys to pile up firewood for him, so he can get through the winter. I have taken firewood to him. People say he knows all the answers to questions of life and death."

"Do you want to go up there?" asked Jesse.

"I met him one time," said Many Roads. "He is a strange old man. He left an impression on me. But we will come here another time, when we can stay and speak with him at leisure. There will be hunting and gathering going on in the valley right now. I would like to be there to help with the work. We will return to visit the hermit after the harvest." He turned into the trail and began the descent into the valley.

They reached the upper end of Mirror Lake by midday, hot and thirsty as To-ko-ya had been when he walked down from the high country. But this time the lake was not dry. They drank, then stripped and swam in the lake to cool themselves. Refreshed, they gathered their belongings and continued along the trail through the pine forest beside the lake shore, toward Ahwahnee. As they walked Many Roads began a story. "Beside this trail, at the other end of this lake where the stream leaves the lake and continues down the canyon, there is a large boulder standing, two times as tall as a man. Long ago, a boy wandered here and as he passed that boulder a grizzly bear appeared from behind it. Arrows have no effect on a grizzly bear. And a spear is not much use. The bear attacked the boy, who fought the grizzly with his knife."

They had come within sight of the boulder in the story. And Many Roads stopped and pointed. "There. That is the boulder." The boulder was still several hundred yards ahead of them, to the right of the trail. As Many Roads spoke a grizzly bear appeared from behind the boulder and looked at them. He stood up on his hind legs, twice the height of a man, and 1500 pounds! He roared, and his scream was blood chilling. He dropped onto all fours and came for them at a clumsy lope.

Many Roads pointed to a trail going uphill through the pine forest to their right. "Run," he said. "Follow it is far as you can, then climb. Fast!"

Jesse needed no urging. He lit out at a run, up the trail. In a hundred yards the trail ended at a boulder choked cleft in the granite cliff face. It was barely wide enough for his body to enter. There were plenty of hand holds. He scrambled up fast, as high as he could go. Suddenly there was a rocky ledge on his left. He scrambled out onto the ledge. Many Roads was right behind him. And the bear was at the foot of the cleft, about forty feet below them, standing on his hind legs, waving his front paws at them and bellowing in a fit of rage. His screams, as they later learned, were heard all over the valley. And people were frightened.

"We're treed," observed Jesse. "What now?"

"I told you we know how to kill grizzlies," answered Many Roads, "If they don't kill us first. As I said, arrows and spears are no good. Some people have killed grizzlies with a knife. But they were also mangled or killed. The best way to escape from a grizzly is to climb. He cannot climb very far up a tree. And he cannot climb steep rock. This is the best way to kill him." With that he began to roll and push large stones over the edge of the shelf, sitting on the ground and using his feet to push, for greater strength. Jesse joined in the exercise. The bear screamed in rage, then was suddenly silent. The boys looked over the ledge and saw the bear lying dead at the foot of the rock wall, victim of one of the falling stones.

"What happened to the boy in the story?" asked Jesse. "The one who fought the bear with his knife?"

"He fought the bear with his knife, though he was badly mauled." answered Many Roads. "He was finally able to climb the rocks and push rocks down and killed the bear. That is how we learned this method of killing grizzlies. We got lucky today. I am glad we saw him before we got to the boulder. We have many black bears here. They are harmless. But grizzly bears are rare in our valley. When they come here from the high country, we kill them right away. Or they will stalk and kill our people."

They climbed down and returned to the trail into the valley. As they left the mouth of the canyon, they came on a gentle river flowing from their left. "This is The River," said Many Roads. Their trail followed The River into the heart of the valley. They came out of the forest into a lush grassy meadow, half a mile across, with hundreds of deer grazing. Jesse looked to his right and saw the two tiers of Yosemite Falls. He had been here before. This was Yosemite Valley. But there were paved roads, tourist busses, a grocery store, none of which were here now. How could this be?

"That is 'The Waterfall'," said Many Roads, pointing to Yosemite Falls. "The village of our chief is near the base of The Waterfall. There are about thirty small villages, all over the valley. There are ten waterfalls, with one or more villages near each. There are several small villages along the river. Most of the villages are Paiute. But Chief Tenaya has a kind heart. He has made people from other tribes welcome to live here. Some have lost their families, some are sick, or they are old and have no one to care for them. Tenaya makes them welcome here. Some of the villages are people from other tribes. But we all live here as one tribe. This valley is called Ahwahnee, meaning 'Deep Grassy Valley.' We call ourselves 'Ahwahneechees,' meaning people who live in Ahwahnee. So we are again one tribe, the Ahwahneechee tribe. Let us visit Chief Tenaya and tell him of the grizzly," said Many Roads. "He will want to send a group to skin it and distribute the meat."

They followed The River through the meadow to a place where a stream flowed into The River from their right. The trail crossed the stream and continued along The River. Another trail branched off and followed alongside the stream through a pine forest toward The Waterfall, from which it flowed. After about a quarter mile, the trail veered away from the stream and came out of the trees into a wide clearing at the base of the vertical granite wall. In the clearing was a village of about twenty wooden teepees, or ochums, all facing east. They were round at the base and pointed on top. They were made of a pole framework that was covered with slabs of bark, instead of buffalo hide like the teepees of the plains tribes. In front of one of these teepees, seated on a log, was chief Tenaya. He rose when he saw Many Roads. "Son, my heart leaps to see you," he said. "You look strong and healthy. I am glad to see you with us again. I am anxious to hear of your travels."

"I am happy to be here for the acorn harvest," replied Many Roads. "Before we talk, let me tell you of a grizzly bear that we killed this afternoon, by Mirror Lake. Perhaps you can send some people to skin it and bring it down."

"I heard his screams above the sound of The Waterfall," said Tenaya. "Scouts were sent to find him and track him. You killed him? Are you injured? Where is he?"

"We encountered him by the boulder where the boy was attacked by a grizzly long ago," answered Many Roads. "We ran up a trail and climbed the wall to a ledge. He followed us, so we pushed rocks down on him and killed him. He lies at the foot of the wall where he died."

"I will send a party to bring him down," said Tenaya.

"While you attend to the bear," said Many Roads, "we will soak in the stream and have a nap. We will join you later for dinner and some stories."

As they walked through the forest toward the stream, Jesse said "Chief Tenaya called you 'son.' The Mojave Chief Pumpkin Eater said you would make a fine chief one day. Are you Chief Tenaya's son?"

"Yes," said Many Roads. "I am son number three. I have two older brothers. We live in a small village on this side of The River near the western end of the valley. The village is mostly young unmarried men and boys. It is close to the only western entrance to the valley. No one but our people use that entrance. Sometimes we go down to the foothills to trade with other tribes, or scouts go down to gather information for Chief Tenaya. There is no trail in the canyon, to make it easy for others. There are just rocks. We walk on the rocks and leave no trail, coming or going. The young men who live in my village are entrusted with the task of watching the approach to the entrance. If anyone comes close, we push rocks down on them, as we did to the grizzly, but much higher. No one has ever continued into the valley once we pushed rocks down on them. Tonight we will dine and sleep in my father's village. There is much to talk about."

They arrived at the stream near the base of The Waterfall and had a refreshing dip in a cold pool. Then they found a place atop a flat granite boulder, warmed by the sun, to dry themselves and have a nap beneath the pines. When they woke to the sweet scent of the pines it was late afternoon and the light had begun to fade. They returned to Chief Tenaya's village to find Many Roads' brothers, his mother and others of his close family, gathered in a circle around a fire. Tenaya was seated on his log where he had been when Jesse first saw him. Among the group was a skinny, wrinkled old squaw, in a soft deerskin dress. Jesse thought she reminded him of pictures of Egyptian mummies. Her skin was dark and shiny like old leather. Her long hair was silver white, her deep set black eyes stared into the distance at things others could not see. She was silent and did not say a word all evening.

The boys joined the group. And everyone welcomed Many Roads back from his travels. A meal was served, of boiled acorn porridge and smoked trout, with a salad of watercress and other assorted greens, dried mushrooms and wild berries.

Then Tenaya produced a cone shaped clay pipe, filled it with dried hemp flowers, lit it and inhaled a puff of smoke. He passed the pipe to Grandmother, seated by his knee. She puffed and passed the pipe, which continued around the circle. "You killed the grizzly bear, Many Roads," announced Chief Tenaya. "He is yours. What shall be done with the rug and the meat?"

"Since you already have two grizzly rugs in your house, I will keep this rug," answered Many Roads, "for the house I share with my brothers. The first one of us to marry will take the rug. The meat can be dispersed as you wish."

"Very well. We would like to hear of your travels," said Tenaya. "Where did you wander? What have you seen? What adventures did you survive? I see a cougar claw on your neck."

"I wandered as far as northern Arizona, Apache lands," began Many Roads, "where all the rocks and the sand are red, where the wind and rains have carved the red hills and canyons into every imaginable shape." He talked late into the night, with his family hanging on every word. They were astonished to hear of his adventure killing the cougar that attacked them, the taming of the treacherous Yumas, the night trek through the sand dunes, and of the killing of the grizzly bear by Mirror Lake. One by one, the older people grew tired and went to their teepees. But the children stayed and listened until they fell asleep on the earth beside the fire. Finally only Many Roads and Jesse were still awake.

"Who is the old woman with the wrinkles?" asked Jesse. "She never spoke a word all evening."

"We call her 'Grandmother'," answered Many Roads. "No one knows who she is. She has always been here, and she has always looked very old and wrinkled. Tenaya's father and grandfather, and all the oldest among us, say that she has always been here and has always looked old and wrinkled, as far back as they can remember, even when they were children. Some say she is the mother of all Paiutes. Some say she is mother of these mountains. She rarely speaks. Few people have heard her speak. When she speaks, her words carry great meaning. She stays here in Tenaya's village. Everyone contributes to her care."

Many Roads added wood to the fire and he and Jesse stretched out on the ground among the children and were soon asleep.

Chapter Seventeen

The next morning Many Roads and Jesse had a breakfast of smoked trout and wild grapes with Chief Tenaya. "There are too many rabbits," spoke Tenaya, "Tomorrow there will be a rabbit drive in the big grassy meadow across the river."

"We will help," said Many Roads. "I returned with the hope of being able to join the autumn hunting and gathering."

"You made a good beginning," said Tenaya. "The grizzly bear will feed many people. We are waiting for the first good windstorm of the season, to blow the acorns from the trees so we can gather our winter acorn supply."

"Good," said Many Roads. "I wanted to join the acorn harvest. I love to walk in the black oak forest in the autumn gathering acorns. We have spent the week in the Tuolumne with Fox Shadow's tribe gathering pine nuts. I will be happy to join the acorn harvest. If there is no hunt or gathering today, I will take a walk around the valley with Lion Catcher."

"When you are at the west end," said Tenaya, "have a look at our defenses above the entrance. There is trouble with the white men. I receive word every few days telling that they have been killing Indians everywhere in these mountains, stealing women and children for slaves, cutting down food trees, killing game and destroying the streams. The Indian tribes north and south of us have gathered in councils and agreed that the white men must be driven out of our mountains. Indians are now killing white men everywhere in an effort to drive them out of the mountains. But the whites keep coming, they keep killing. There are too many of them. They drive whole villages out of the

Paiute Teepee Village on The River in Ahwahnee

mountains to the hot valley below and put them in pens like horses. We have remained uninvolved and have not made war on the whites. We may be safe here, in our hidden valley. They may never discover our valley. If they do, the west entrance along the river is the only way in. They will never find the east entrance from Tuolumne. We may have to defend the west entrance. So have a look at our preparations there. And tell me if you see ways to improve our defenses."

"I will do as you ask," answered Many Roads.

The boys set out walking west along the north side of The River, sometimes through grassy meadows, other times among sweet scented pines, or through tall forests of black oak. They stopped to swim in The River and dry themselves lying naked in the sun, in the grass on the bank among the wildflowers.

Occasionally they passed a small village of wooden teepees. At one point Many Roads saw a plant he recognized and stopped to gather a small quantity of the bulbous roots from beneath the long, narrow wavy green sword shaped leaves. "These are called 'soap root.' You can peel off the layers of the root and use them for cleaning things or washing away blood or fat," said Many Roads. "Later I will show you another use for them."

As they passed another small village of wooden teepees set in the shade beneath the pines at the base of the granite north wall, Many Roads said "This is the village where I stay with my brothers. I don't stay here very much, since I wander a lot." As they crossed a small stream that flowed into The River, he pointed to a boy fishing with poised spear. "He lives in this village."

To-tu'-ya, a Paiute Maid, Gathering Wild Grapes in Ahwahnee

"This valley is a beautiful place," remarked Jesse. "It might be the most beautiful place on the earth, as you have said."

Many Roads pointed across the valley to a tall thin gossamer waterfall, waving gently back and forth in the breezes, like a ribbon of silk. "That is Puffing Wind Waterfall (Bridalveil Fall)," he said. "There is a village at the base of the fall and one on the stream that flows from it to The River, and yet another where the stream flows into The River, and another near the headwaters of the stream, above the waterfall. There are many small villages all over the valley."

As they walked, Jesse saw groups of ten or twenty children of all ages picking berries or wild fruit into wicker baskets. "From the time we can walk," said Many Roads, "during summer and autumn, all the children in a village will often spend the day playing and swimming together in groups. The older ones watch out for the little ones. Each child carries a basket and they all pick berries and fruit during the day, to bring back to the village at day's end."

The walk was a sojourn in heaven for Jesse. After weeks in the desert, this lush green valley was just like the place Jesse's old grandmother used to tell him you go when you die. Whether he was dead or alive, he was very happy to be here. He had loved Yosemite and wanted to return here one day. Now he was enjoying it as a guest of the culture that lived in the valley as their mountain home, with no reason to ever leave. What a wonderful thought. He had slowly begun to realize that he was no longer in his own time. He was living in a page from history. He did not know what had happened or how it came to be that he was here and no longer with his family. Perhaps he had died, and this was really heaven, or something like it. But he knew he would be happy to live here in this valley forever.

They had come five miles or more from Tenaya's village. Many Roads followed a trail that now left the forest and began to climb high along the northern wall of a granite gorge a mile deep. The River they had been following plunged down the rocks, following the canyon out of the mountains into the foothills and then into the California central valley. They could see down the treeless canyon for many miles. Anyone approaching the valley must come this way, along The River in the canyon bottom, over rugged rocky terrain with no trail and no cover.

Soon their path widened and they came onto a very large shelf, several hundred feet wide and a half mile long across the face of the granite mountain, open and bare, but for piles of boulders and stones, and a stand of pine trees. Jesse could see several wooden teepees among the pines. There was a row of large rocks and boulders lined up along the lip of the shelf, ready for pushing over to fall on intruders far below. Lying near the rocks were sturdy pry poles to use as levers.

Many Roads' brothers were there and several other Indian youths. These were the door wards, the sentinels who watched and guarded the entrance to the hidden valley.

When Jesse looked over the edge, far below he could see a talus slope and below that the river. Rocks being pushed off the ledge would bounce down the mountainside a thousand feet or more, and crash into the talus slope below causing a rockslide that might sweep an army into The River. This appeared to be a very good way to protect the privacy of this valley.

Many Roads and Jesse shared a meal of roasted quail and trout with the brothers, then headed back to the valley to continue their walk. After re-entering the forest they backtracked for a short distance, then took a path toward The River. When they reached The River, Many Roads swam across, holding his bow and arrows above the water with one hand. The River was a gentle one, for its entire length, being only a couple of hundred feet wide and shallow. It was crystal clear, fed by snow melt from the high country, and clean enough to drink. Jesse followed Many Roads across The River. They continued their walk on the south side of The River, returning east now, back toward Tenaya's village but on the opposite side of the river.

Not far beyond the stream that flowed down from Puffing Wind Waterfall, Many Roads stopped and pointed back across the valley to a mile high stone monolith that was part of the north wall. "See that big rock?" he asked. "That is 'Rock Chief' (El Capitan). You see the long nose and the two eyes? The whole rock is a big chief's head, with the face eternally watching the west entrance to the valley. That face looks like Tenaya."

As Many Roads spoke, Jesse suddenly saw the face on the rock! The rock was a huge head and face, watching the west end of the valley! Many Roads pointed to the east of Rock Chief, to a cluster of three gigantic pointed rocks close together in a row. "Those rocks we call 'Three Frogs Copulating' (The Three Brothers)."

The Ahwahneechees were seemingly living in a huge rock garden. Everywhere they looked, all around the valley, all the prominent landmarks were personified. Wherever the people looked they saw living images in the rocks that were their role models,

"Rock Chief" now named El Capitan

"Three Frogs Copulating" now named The Three Brothers

companions, protectors. They remembered stories in the waters that taught them how to be good people and live good lives. They learned their very morals and ethics from the stories handed down, generation to generation, about the rocks and waters here. All their lives they would think of those stories every time they looked up and saw one of the rocks or waterfalls. Their roots went deep, their culture was ancient, they were intimately connected to their valley home in ways the white people could never see or understand.

The trail continued to wander east through black oak forests, pine forests and wide sunlit, grassy meadows thick with herds of hundreds of deer and elk. Small black bears wandered freely. Sometimes Jesse would look up and see the round ball of a black bear in the crotch of a tree, napping. Every now and then, Jesse would see another waterfall he had not seen before. And The Waterfall near Tenaya's village was visible from almost everywhere on the valley floor. The granite rocks that made the walls of the valley soared vertically a mile above their heads. Some of the waterfalls were half a mile high. To describe this place to someone who had never seen it might severely damage your credibility. People would think you exaggerated fantastically and would not believe you by half.

As they drew close to Tenaya's village, Many Roads cut across a wide grassy meadow. When they reached The River, he found a long, wide still pool, where the water was shallow and not more than chest deep. Many Roads moved around to the head of the pool, where water from upstream rippled over the rocks into the pool. He removed the soap root from his pouch and laid the bulbs on the rocks. He picked up a fist size stone and began to crush the bulbous roots. He tossed two of the crushed roots to

Jesse. He took other roots in his hands and immersed them in the stream, squeezing them to release their juices into the stream water flowing into the pool. Jesse did likewise. Foamy bubbles like soap bubbles appeared on the surface of the pool.

"The juice from these roots will flow through the pool and stun the fish," explained Many Roads. "They will float to the surface and down to the far end of the pool. We will wait there to gather them." He rose and walked along the river bank to the far end of the pool, where he sat down in the grass to wait.

Pretty soon, Jesse saw fish begin to float to the surface of the pool. Many Roads plunged into the pool and began to gather and toss fish onto the grassy bank. Jesse followed suit. Altogether, the boys gathered more than thirty fine trout.

When they left the water, they gathered the fish and Many Roads cut two thin switches thick as your finger from a shrub growing by the water's edge. He trimmed them to about three feet long, leaving one three inch twig projecting at the end for a retaining hook. He then picked up one of the trout and pushed the other end of the stick through one of the fish's gills and out the fish's mouth. He strung them one after the other until the stick was strung full of fish. Jesse copied his motions. And they soon had two fat strings of fine trout. "These will make a welcome addition to dinner this evening," ventured Many Roads.

String of Mountain Brook Trout

Yosemite Valley by Thomas Hill

Chapter Eighteen

That evening they enjoyed another family dinner by the fire in front of Tenaya's log. They dined on acorn mush, smoked trout and a salad of mixed greens and wild fruit. They shared stories, this night with Many Roads hearing of events in the valley while he was away, who was married, who was born, who had died. Again, Chief Tenaya spoke of the white men in the west and of the trouble they were bringing to the mountains. He was worried. He spoke of a village in The River canyon, forty miles from the mouth of the valley, where mounted white men had attacked and driven all the people out of their teepees. Some were killed. The houses and food stores were burned and the people driven like animals to a reservation in the San Joaquin Valley, where they were penned like horses and cattle.

"Many Roads," spoke Tenaya, "Consider places that we might hide all of our people if the white men ever discover our valley. Let us choose the best places and construct chuck-ahs to store food. We should prepare, so that we have a safe place to lead the people if the white men come here." It was the first time that those who listened ever heard their chief speak as if the white men might actually find and enter Ahwahnee.

"There is a ledge on the north wall of the canyon," replied Many Roads. "Not far from the place where we killed the grizzly. It is a steep climb up a rocky cleft. I think everyone can make it up there. I don't know about Grandmother. Maybe she can be carried. The path is over rock and would leave no tracks for them to follow. The shelf is large enough to hold many people. There are pine trees, there is a spring for water. There is only one way up onto the ledge. If anyone tried to climb up, we could push rocks over as we did with the grizzly. With food and water, many people could stay up there for a long time."

"I know the place," said Tenaya. "It affords a good view of the valley, so we could watch their movements. Yes, I like that choice. We can move some food up there and build chuck-ahs to store it. If we have to live up there for awhile, the food will be on hand. The white men won't have enough food to stay here long. After they leave, we can return to the valley. If they burn our teepees, we can make more. Perhaps we should move all of our food stores to our hiding places, so the white men will not be able to destroy our winter food."

"Another place of choice," offered Many Roads, "would be up in the end of Arrowwood Canyon (Indian Canyon), south of the lake. There is a small hidden canyon, hard to find unless you know the way in. It can hold many people. It is sheltered from the wind and storms. There is water, and pine forests to hide in. We can build chuck-ahs and store food there, as well."

The boys slept by Tenaya's fire that night. Next morning after breakfast, all the squaws and children in the village gathered and walked down to the river and waded across a shallow rocky place. Most of them carried striking sticks. Some of the boys carried bundles of rolled up rabbit nets. They all stopped on the edge of the wide meadow. All of the boys carried the nets to the far end of the meadow and began setting them up with sticks, as a barrier hundreds of yards long across the end of the meadow. The net was made of cord from twisted plant fibers. The old men of the tribe spent the winter months in their teepees making the rabbit nets for younger, more agile hunters to use. It had a three inch mesh and was about three feet high. Each section was about a hundred feet long. They were attached end to end, and stretched across the meadow.

Once the net was set up the boys waved to the women and children at the other end of the meadow, a half mile away. One of the women directed everyone to spread out in a long line across the meadow. Then they all began to advance through the grass toward the boys and the net at the far end of the meadow, beating the grass with sticks and making joyful noise as they went. As they moved along, all the rabbits hidden in the grass became frightened and moved away from the advancing line. They were slowly driven the length of the meadow until they ran headlong into the nets and were tangled. The boys were waiting with striking sticks and killed the rabbits as fast as they arrived.

Once the women and children arrived at the net and there were no more rabbits, the group began to gather the dead rabbits and tie their feet together in bunches, for carrying back to the village. It was a successful rabbit drive. The meat would feed many mouths, and the furs would make blankets to keep people warm in the coming winter.

The boys spent their days exploring the valley, and all its nooks and crannies. They often followed The River up the south canyon, climbed Sparkling Waterfall (Vernal Falls) and Twisting Waterfall (Nevada Falls) to explore Little Ahwahnee (Little Yosemite Valley), a smaller valley with cliffs, forests, meadows, streams and The River, as beautiful as Ahwahnee itself. They lingered in beautiful places. And when people were hunting and gathering, the boys joined in and helped with the work, shared in the camaraderie.

A week after the rabbit drive, there came a day when heavy autumn winds swept over the valley for three days. When the calm that followed settled in, the people were ready for the acorn harvest. No one announced it. No one sent out notice for everyone to gather for the harvest. Everyone just knew that the first heavy windstorm of autumn would shake the acorns from the trees and it would be time to gather them from the forest floor.

On the third day after the wind had passed, people from all the villages in the valley gathered in the black oak forests everywhere. Everyone carried burden baskets to gather the acorns. The people worked in lines that moved through the forest, like the line of rabbit hunters moving through the meadow grass. As they went over the carpet of oak leaves, they stooped and picked up every acorn they could see and put them in the burden baskets. When the baskets were filled, some of the workers took them to large chuck-ahs, storage shelters, like tiny silos on stilts, with the roof and sides covered with a thatch of pine boughs with the needles pointing downward, to keep out squirrels and mice. Some of the acorns were processed for more immediate use. These were spread out on the tops of flat granite boulders and beaten with sticks to crack the shells. Then they were left lying in the sun for several days. This would cause the cracks to open wider. Then the people would come and pick the acorn nuts from the shells.

To prepare the acorns for eating, they would be crushed into a coarse meal, using stone pestles in ancient mortar holes in the flat, smooth tops of boulders. As Jesse had wandered and become familiar with the valley and its surroundings, he had seen several places where there were flat topped boulders with

Milling Boulder with Mortar Holes for Grinding Acorns

groups of holes, several inches wide and several inches deep, where hundreds of generations of Indian women had ground acorns. The acorns were ground into a fine meal or flour, which was placed into a sieve and water poured through the meal until the water came out clear. This is to leach out bitter flavors in the raw acorns. Then the leached meal is ready to use.

To cook it, the acorn meal is placed in a cooking basket and covered with water. Stones are heated red hot in a fire and picked up with green sticks and placed into the acorn meal. The hot stones bring the mush to a boil. And it is ready to eat.

Many Roads and Jesse spent the days of late summer and autumn exploring the canyons and valleys in the mountains. They hunted and fished, joined in village hunting and gathering activities, they swam in the rivers and streams, climbed the peaks, frolicked in the sunshine, dozed in the green meadows, and at night slept on the earth beneath the open sky. The autumn advanced. The first snow of the approaching winter fell in the valley. If possible, the valley became more beautiful than before, an ice and snow dusted fantasyland. The sun came out again and melted most of the snow, except for little pockets here and there hidden in shady places. They had weeks more of mild sunny weather, a true Indian summer, that the tribe used for more hunting and gathering and piling up of firewood. Indians don't cut live trees for firewood. They harvest the dead limbs and trees that have fallen to the forest floor, leaving the living tree to produce food nuts and more firewood.

Then more snow came, and the valley took on its winter cloak. The people retreated to their teepees and caves, where they worked making baskets, rabbit nets, fur blankets and arrows, and deerskin clothing. One of the squaws made a short, hip-length rabbit skin cape for Jesse. It tied at the throat and draped over his shoulders. Sitting cross-legged on the ground, he could gather it around himself to keep warm. It was silky soft. He had long since given up his cargo shorts and T-shirt for a deerskin loincloth. As the weather grew cold, many of the men began wearing deerskin shirts, and the squaws wore deerskin dresses. Many Roads gave Jesse a soft deerskin shirt. He still wore his hi-tech sandals. His skin was dark from the desert and mountain sunshine, and his hair was long to his shoulders, with a pair of red-tail hawk feathers tied on one side. If you didn't look too close he might pass for an Indian.

Jesse had become an Ahwahneechee. He was pleased with that and by now had completely accepted that he would be living here for the rest of his life.

Jesse was happy hunting and fishing with Many Roads. Even in winter they still took long walks and continued to explore the canyons and valleys and to enjoy the wonderland that winter had made of the valley. The valley was deep enough to be sheltered from the worst of the violence from the mountain storms. Winters in the valley were gentler than in the high country.

All through the winter, Chief Tenaya continued to receive reports about the violence between white men and Indians. He knew that the white men had learned the location of the valley. They were determined to drive all Indians out of the mountains. And they were coming. Preparations had been made, hiding places selected and stocked with food stores. People in all the villages had been notified and were aware of these locations. But the people did not believe that the white men would ever find or enter their valley. And those who were young and strong said that if the whites did come, they would hide and avoid them. "We can find plenty of food in these mountains."

The boys lived for days at a time with the other young men on the ledge watching the western river approach to the valley. One day they saw a large group of mounted men approaching along The River, still two miles or more away. A single rider was riding point, about a quarter mile in advance of the main body. As the single horseman came below the ledge, the boys pushed one of the smaller rocks over the edge. As Jesse watched, it fell and it bounced off the mountainside, again and again, dislodging stones as it went and creating a deadly rockslide. The horse and rider were swept into The River and disappeared from sight. The other horsemen stopped, then reversed their course and returned the way they had come.

On another day, they saw a single traveler coming along The River. They guessed it might be an Indian, maybe even one of their own. So they did not send stones down on his head, but continued to watch as he climbed the rocks higher and higher toward the valley entrance. Many Roads and Jesse went to meet him as he entered the valley.

This was an Indian, though from a different tribe, one of the tribes that lived in the western foothills. He said that he was sent from the white men with a message for Chief Tenaya. The boys decided to escort him to the chief. When they arrived at Chief Tenaya's village, they found the old chief sitting on his log. The messenger approached the chief and said: "I have a message from the leader of the white army that hunts Indians in these mountains. He said that if you come out of the mountains voluntarily to reservations in the plains, you will be given food, clothing and blankets. You will be protected. If you do not come, the white men will come into your valley and exterminate your whole tribe. Not one of you will be left alive."

"Thank you for bringing this message," replied Chief Tenaya. "You must be tired and hungry. One of the squaws will bring you food and show you a place where you can sleep. When you wake you may return to the white men tomorrow, if you wish. Or you may stay with us here in the valley."

Three more times messengers came into the valley, always with the same message. Finally, Tenaya decided to go himself down to the white men's camp and try to negotiate with them. At the very least he might inform himself regarding their strength and resources.

Chapter Nineteen

In the summer and autumn of 1850, The Indian 'problem' in the Sierra Nevada Mountains was pretty much solved. The Mariposa Battalion, a mounted and armed force of 200 miners and traders, had been commissioned and financed by the State of California and authorized to enter the mountains for the expressed purpose of killing or capturing all Indians living in the 500 mile long mountain range and removing them to reservations in the central valley. By winter all tribes had been subjugated except the Ahwahneechees in Yosemite Valley. Plans were laid to enter the valley in the spring. Indian messengers from other tribes were sent into the valley with messages for Chief Tenaya, telling him that if he would bring his people out of the mountains voluntarily to reservations on the Fresno River, they would not be killed and would be given food and blankets and clothing. If they did not comply, they would be exterminated, and not one of them would be left alive.

Some of the messengers actually made it into the valley. Most of those decided to stay. It was much nicer than the reservation. There was plenty to eat. And the people were nicer and kinder than the whites.

By March of 1851, The Mariposa Battalion, heavily armed and fully supplied, left Mariposa, California and journeyed up The River determined to find the valley and deal with the recalcitrant Ahwahneechees. They established a camp on The River east of Mariposa. A special envoy was sent to Chief Tenaya in Ahwahnee, telling him again that if he would bring his people out to the reservation, they would be given food, clothing and blankets, and they would be protected. If they would not come, the white men would come to their valley and kill them all.

Chief Tenaya, fearing for his people, decided to make an effort to negotiate with the whites. He left the mountains and went, with a small escort, to the camp of the Mariposa Battalion. He left the escort in a hidden location, so they could watch, and escape if there was treachery. Then he approached the camp alone. Once in sight of the camp, he stopped and stood motionless until he was seen and approached by an Indian scout from a different tribe. He was recognized, and the leader of the group, a trader by the name of James Savage, was informed of his presence and came to meet him. Savage lead Tenaya into the camp. He told Tenaya that if he would meet with representatives of the government and make a treaty, the whites would not make war on the Ahwahneechees, and they would be given gifts. If they would not cooperate, they would all be killed.

Tenaya spoke: "My people do not want anything from the white men. The Great Spirit is our father and has always supplied us with all we need. We do not want anything from the white men. Go, then. Leave us in these mountains where we were born, where the ashes of our fathers have been given to the winds. We are willing to live in peace with the white men. We have not made war on you. But my people do not want to go to the plains. We will stay in our valley in the mountains. I have said enough!"

Savage tried again to threaten the old chief. "You must meet with the government and make a treaty," he insisted. "If you do not, your whole tribe will be destroyed. Not one of them will be left alive."

Tenaya had seen the many horses and weapons, and the hard determined faces and gross behavior of the white men. He understood now that there was little hope for the tribe to remain in their mountain valley. He saw that the whites had the numbers and the resources to invade the valley and exterminate the Ahwahneechees. He suddenly felt very old and tired. "I will not lie to you," he said. "If allowed to return to my people, I will bring them out of the mountains."

"We will go with you to bring them," Savage responded.

"The snow is too deep for your horses," said the chief. "Even if you got through the snow, at the entrance to our valley the rocks are steep. Your horses might get safely down into the valley and out again. But they would be more likely to founder or fall. You would be likely to lose horses and men. You would be trapped in heavy snow, with insufficient supplies. You would have to walk out on foot through the deep snow."

"How long will it take for your people to get here?" asked Savage.

"It depends on the snow," replied the chief.

"I believe you lie to me," said Savage. "All Indians are no more than vermin and cannot be trusted. But I will let you go. If you do not bring your people, I will come to your valley and they will come with me, or die."

The old chief left the camp and rejoined his escort. They returned to the valley, where Tenaya called a council of all the village leaders. He conveyed the message from Savage and told the people what he had seen in their camp, of the horses and weapons and hard faces. He told them that he believed the white men would soon come to their valley and that they would all be killed if they refused to leave the valley and go to the reservation in the plains. "I will go," he said. "Any who believe my words and wish to go with me should be ready to leave tomorrow morning. Take all the food and blankets you can carry. Those who stay should keep a constant watch. Hide on the ledge until they have left."

The following morning, Tenaya, concerned that Savage might be already on his way to the valley, left by himself at dawn for the white men's camp, leaving instructions for the others to follow as soon as they were prepared. He walked to the white men's camp by himself, in deep sadness, understanding that this was the end of his tribe and their way of life, the end of their beloved deep grassy valley. His aim now was to save their lives.

When he arrived at the camp, he informed Savage that the tribe was en route and would arrive in due time. Savage was openly suspicious. When the villagers did not arrive by dark, he became hostile. When the Ahwahneechees had not shown up the next morning, the Mariposa Battalion mounted and set out for Yosemite Valley to bring them in. Tenaya was presented with a saddled horse and joined the white men. As the group reached the mouth of the valley they met the Ahwahneechees on their way to the white camp. Savage counted seventy-two Indians. "This cannot be all of your people," he said to Tenaya.

"You will not find any of my people," replied Tenaya. "I do not know where they are. We are a small tribe. I have talked with my people and told them that I would go meet with the white chiefs and make peace. Some said that I am growing old and that it is good that I should go. They said that young and strong men can find plenty to eat in the mountains. Therefore, why should they go to the plains to be yarded like horses and cattle? My heart has been sore since this talk. But I am willing to go now. It is best for my people that I do so. This is all of my people that will go down to the plains."

Savage sent a guard with the Indians, to make sure they continued to the white camp. Then he took the main body of men into the valley and made a camp not far from Puffing Wind Waterfall. He expressed his intentions to search the valley for other Indians before the day was gone. But when his group tried to ford The River, swollen by snowmelt, some of their horses were swept off their feet and their riders soaked in the icy waters. So the group returned to their camp, built huge bonfires and spent the rest of the day trying to dry themselves and their clothing. Next morning the white men set out to search the valley.

The white men searched everywhere. Yet they could not find any Indians. Everywhere they searched they found recently abandoned villages, but no Indians. When they found a village, they burned the teepees and chuck-ahs containing food stores. Tenaya had not yet moved all the food to the hiding places. So the Ahwahneechees lost a significant part of their winter food stores to the invaders.

When they found and entered Tenaya's village, they found one Indian. Grandmother was seated on the ground tending a small fire. The white men were astonished to see the wrinkled old woman sitting calmly by the fire. At first she ignored them and did not seem to notice their presence. "Where are the others?" they asked her.

"If you want to find them," she said, "go look for them."

"Who are you?" they asked. "Why are you here alone?"

"I am too old to run and hide," she answered. After that, they could not get another word out of her. She sat staring into her little fire and would not speak.

The white men told her that she must come with them. But she sat in silence, ignoring them as though they were not even there. As the white men approached Grandmother, intent on laying hands on her, suddenly a sphere of bright light appeared all around her, enclosing her. The light from the sphere grew brighter and contained all the colors of the rainbow. The sphere began to expand slowly and grew larger. As the surface of the sphere drew near the white men, each one screamed in fear and ran away from the expanding globe of light. Then the light and colors in the sphere began to fade, the sphere became diffuse and then dissolved and disappeared altogether. As the white men approached Grandmother, they found her dead, her lifeless body lying on the ground beside the fire.

Savage's efforts to find Indians were frustrated. The Indians that he could not find were hiding up on the ledge on the north canyon wall, watching the white men destroy their homes and food.

After they had burned everything they could find of the Indians' houses and food stores, the white men left the valley and returned to their camp on The River. The people came down from the ledge and began to build new teepees. There was some food left, up on the ledge. But the winter food supply was seriously depleted by the raid. So the people began sifting through the charred remains of the acorns burned by the whites, trying to salvage what they could.

Chapter Twenty

When they had returned to the white camp on The River, the invaders found the seventy-two Indians there, occupied with cooking foods for themselves. With their bows and arrows some of the Indian boys had shot rabbits, squirrels and quail along the way, and one fat deer.

Savage decided to move the Indians to the reservation on the Fresno River the next day. But because his supplies were short, and because he did not want to slow the horsemen down with people on foot, the main body of the Mariposa Battalion left that day for the reservation. Thinking the Indians were now subjugated, Savage left behind a small nine man guard to accompany the seventy-two Indians the following day on the three day walk to the Fresno River.

That night after the guard had gone to sleep, the Ahwahneechees slipped quietly out of the camp and headed back to their valley in the mountains. On waking and finding the Indians gone, the leader of the guard led his men in mounted pursuit. When the Indians saw them coming they scattered in all directions and hid in the grass, in the brush, in ravines and on rocky, brush covered slopes. With only nine men, the whites could not follow every Indian. And they now had to be concerned about being ambushed. Frustrated they left for the reservation to report to Savage. On their arrival at the Fresno River reservation they learned that 350 Indians from other tribes had fled the reservation. The men of the Mariposa Battalion were hunting them all over the San Joaquin Valley and throughout the Sierra foothills. There was no one available to chase the Ahwahneechees.

The Ahwahneecheess returned to their deep grassy valley and began to build new teepees. They sifted through the smoldering ruins of the chuck-ahs and picked out any acorns that were still edible. They removed the burnt shells and kept the scorched acorns for eating. Many acorns were saved, though in a damaged condition. The acorns in the chuck-ahs that were not discovered and burned were moved to the hiding places. The young men once more resumed their watches on the ledge at the valley's mouth.

With their food supplies seriously depleted, the Ahwahneechees would have to rely on fishing and hunting to get through this year to autumn harvest. But there were swarms of fish in The River and streams. And the deer and rabbits were plentiful. And the people were strong. They would survive.

On May 5, 1851, The Mariposa Battalion, better supplied and armed than on their previous visit in March, returned to Yosemite Valley to finish the rape of Ahwahnee. They established their main camp at the location near Puffing Wind Waterfall. Then Savage sent out groups to discover the Indians and to destroy any new teepees. One group of twelve white men were riding in the open along the south side of The River, when they spotted five Indians on the north side of The River just east of the Rock Chief. This was Many Roads, his two brothers, Jesse and one other youth. They were returning from their watch on the ledge. They had seen the white men approaching the valley but Chief Tenaya had instructed them not to push rocks down on them. They were sent to watch the whites and report to Tenaya. Now they were on their way to the ledge where Tenaya was hiding with all the Ahwahneechees, to report to the chief that the white men were now in the valley.

The white men rode their horses into and across The River to pursue them. The boys began to run, but the horses were overtaking them. They turned off the trail near 'Three Frogs' and ran through the trees toward the north wall. Coming out of the trees they encountered the talus slope and began to climb. They climbed very high and hid among the rocks. But the white men spread out below to guard against their escape. Soon their leader sent Indian scouts from other tribes up the talus to tell them to come down, that they would not be harmed and would be given gifts. The scouts showed them the bright colored bandanas and shirts they had received from the whites. The boys did not want the white men's gifts. But they saw no way out, so they surrendered to the whites.

The boys were questioned by the leader of the white men about the whereabouts of Tenaya. They refused to answer. The leader then asked if they could take a message to Tenaya if they were released. Many Roads said they could.

At this time Tenaya and most of the Ahwahneechees were hidden on the ledge on the north wall across the canyon from Tis-sa-ack. The boys were tied and kept prisoner overnight in the white camp. The next day two of the boys were released from their bonds and in company with one of the white men were instructed to find Tenaya and deliver the message that he should bring his people and surrender. That they would be treated fairly and would not be harmed. The white man was instructed to escort and protect the Indians from other white men and to see that they delivered the message to Tenaya.

As they walked on the trail toward Mirror Lake, they were stopped by three white men, one of whom was injured and bloody. One of the men leveled his rifle at one of the Indians and yelled for the white man accompanying the boys to move away. He announced his intentions to kill the two Indians. His party had discovered the hiding place of the Indians and had tried to climb up to the ledge. But the Indians had thrown stones down at them and seriously injured one of them. They were mad and in a vengeful mood.

The escort with the boys refused to move and pushed the two boys behind himself to protect them. He announced that his instructions were to protect the boys and see that they delivered a message to Tenaya. He reasoned calmly with the others until they relaxed and the threat was ended. Then he and the boys continued on their mission. The white man accompanied the two boys to the base of the cliff and permitted them to climb the rock up to the ledge. Then he returned to the white camp.

The men at the camp were having a shooting contest using bows and arrows they had captured from the Indians. Some of the arrows went astray and some went quite a way beyond the target. So Many Roads brother was untied and permitted to go with one white man to retrieve the arrows. Soon he was competing in the shooting contest, and his skill with the bow was superior to any of the white men. They were impressed with his ability. After their initial excitement over the game wore off and the white men lost interest, the brother took a very long shot and intentionally lost the arrow in the distant trees. When he went to retrieve the arrow with the white escort, he found a chance and took off at a run. The white man gave chase, but the Indian was in far better condition and knew the terrain. It wasn't much of a contest. Many Roads brother disappeared.

As a result of the escape, Many Roads and Jesse were tied back to back. A two-man guard was posted to watch the boys and prevent any more escapes. The boys talked quietly with one another. Many Roads said that they should try to untie themselves and try to run into the trees and escape. Jesse agreed. And they began to feel for the knots on the rope that bound them. As they worked, Jesse said "You were showing me the way home. I have come to love this valley and would like to spend the rest of my life here. Maybe this will be my home now, if the white men don't drive us out."

"Have you learned nothing from traveling with me?" asked Many Roads. "Home is not a place on the earth. It is a state of mind. It is something inside you. The Apache word for home is 'kuhn-gan-hay.' This means fire place. 'Home' is wherever the fire is. 'Home' is about how you feel inside. You can feel at home everywhere."

"Yes," said Jesse. "I've learned that, thanks, to you. But this valley is still the most beautiful place on earth. And I will make my home here, as long as I am able."

The white men noticed that the boys were untying their bonds. One of the men got up and started to go tighten the ropes. But the others stopped him. They were still very angry over the man injured by the rocks thrown from the ledge and wanted revenge. "Let them make a run for it," said one man. "We can watch and wait and keep our pistols ready to stop an escape attempt."

So the white men let Many Roads and Jesse untie their ropes and make a run for it. All the men opened fire at the running boys. Many Roads was shot in the back and killed. Jesse was struck a grazing blow on the side of his head and fell unconscious into a dense clump of huckleberry shrubs. The white men did not bother to retrieve the bodies but let them lie where they had fallen.

Chapter Twenty-One

The whites had discovered the hiding place of the Indians on the ledge. They had sent several Indian scouts up with messages urging Tenaya to come down from the ledge, with assurances that he would be treated fairly and neither he nor his people would be hurt.

Tenaya finally came down to parlay with the white men. He simply walked into the camp where the boys had been held. His eyes fell on Many Roads body, still lying in the dirt where he had fallen, on the earth beneath the pines, his blood soaking into the soil of the deep grassy valley. Those who saw Tenaya's quivering lips and the deadly hatred in his eyes stepped back when he turned his gaze on them. He was treated with civility and respect. Savage apologized for the death of his son. When questioned he refused to speak. Then as Savage tried once more to threaten him, Tenaya faced him:

"Kill me, sir!," spoke Tenaya. "Yes, kill me, as you killed my son! Kill me as you would kill my people if they were to surrender! You would kill all of my race if you could. Yes sir, American, you can now tell your warriors to kill this old chief. You have made me sorrowful, my life dark. You killed the child of my heart. Why not kill the father? All you know is killing and greed. Yes, sir, American. My spirit will make trouble for you and your people, as you have made trouble for me and my people. With the wizards I will follow and make you fear me. You may kill me, sir, but you will not live in peace. I will follow in your footsteps. I will not leave Ahwahnee, but will be with the spirits among the rocks, in the waterfalls, in the rivers and in the winds. You are lost and will never find your way. Wherever you go, I will be with you, confounding you. You will not see me, but you will fear the spirit of this old chief and grow cold. The Great Spirits have spoken! I am done!"

The Ahwahneechees were finally driven from Yosemite Valley and were scattered to the four winds, fulfilling a prophecy Teneya had heard long ago: "If a white man ever sets foot in Ahwahnee, your people will be driven forth and scattered." Some went to reservations, some went to live with the Mono Paiutes, some went to live with other Indians all over California and Nevada. A few even returned to Ahwahnee to live as beggars in their own land, selling trinkets to the tourists who flooded in.

Tenaya went to live on the reservation in the San Joaquin Valley. After only a few months, he gathered his family and returned to Ahwahnee. A small number of Ahwahneechees joined him. Shortly after his return to the valley, a group of Mono Paiutes attacked the Ahwahneechees. Tenaya was killed by a blow to the head from a stone thrown by a jealous young Mono chief.

On July 1, 1851, the Mariposa Battalion was disbanded. James Savage engaged in trading and ranching. Bad blood developed between him and many of the settlers along the King's River, including a Tulare County judge, Major Harvey. On August 16, 1852, during an argument, Savage was shot and killed by the judge. No charges were brought, since the killing was seen as justifiable, in view of Savage's history of aggression and violence.

Rock Chief, Spirit of Tenaya
Eternally Watching the West Entrance to Ahwahnee

Epilogue

When Jesse opened his eyes he found himself in a hospital bed. His mom and dad were sitting in chairs by the window, talking in quiet voices. And his sister, Sam, was sitting in a chair watching TV. He is confused. "Where am I?" he asked. His parents, startled, are glad to see him awake. They rise and move to the side of the bed.

"You are in a hospital, Jesse," said his mom. "You were hurt. But you will be okay, now."

"Where?" asked Jesse.

"In the Grand Canyon. You fell out of the raft and hit your head on a rock. You've been unconscious for three days," his mom replied.

"Where is this hospital?" asked Jesse. "How did I get here?"

"Flagstaff, Arizona," replied his mom. "Search and Rescue flew you here in a helicopter when they found you."

"Where is Many Roads?" asked Jesse.

"What?" replied his mom.

Jesse turned his head away toward the window, disappointed. It was all just a dream. There was no Many Roads, no odyssey. Only three days had passed. It had all been a delirious dream.

Then his sister, Sam, approached the bed. "Where did you get these things, Jesse?" asked Sam, holding up the obsidian knife and the cougar claw that Many Roads had given him.

End

Ahwahnee Paiute Suzie McGowan & Daughter

Spring 2015

On leaving Oliver's Market in Cotati, California, I heard the soft, gentle music of a wooden flute. It was so soothing that I had to stop and to listen, until the music came to and end. Then I approached the flute player, whom I perceived to be a short Native American. In his hands was an Indian wooden flute. I congratulated him and thanked him for the music.

Seeing a box of CDs by his feet, I asked if I could buy one. When he handed it to me I saw the name, Albert Tenaya, on the cover. I asked him if he was related to Chief Tenaya of the Yosemite Ahwahneechees. He told that yes he was descended from the Maria Lebrado, the granddaughter of Chief Tenaya. What an exciting moment that was for me.

I had always believed that all the Ahwahneechees were scattered and absorbed by other tribes all over California, Nevada, Oregon and Idaho. Albert Tenaya told me, also, that between 200 and 300 descendants of Ahwahneechees lived near one another in southern Idaho, and that another 100 lived in Oregon. He said that smaller numbers were scattered around in other places.

I was very happy to learn that The Ahwahneechee tribe still exists today, including their hereditary chief.

Today, Albert Tenaya plays his flute and carries the DNA of the Ahwahneechee people into the future. He can be seen and heard at Indian festivals all over the USA. His CDs can be sampled and purchased at www.alberttenaya.com

Wild Foods

PINE NUTS: *p. sabiniana, p. lambertiana, p. monophylla,* and about 20 other pines have nuts that are useful as human food. All pine nuts are edible, though some are too small to be of practical use as food.

ACORN: more than 60 species of oaks have acorns that are edible. The black oak was choice among California mountain Indians. The California Valley Oak is the favorite of Indians in the foothills and central valley.

BERRIES & FRUIT: manzanita berries, blackberry, strawberry, elderberry, thimbleberry, raspberry, cherry, plum (*prunus subcordata*), wild grape, date.

FISH & GAME: deer, elk, antelope, rabbit, squirrel, black bear, mustang, fish, turkey, quail, pheasant, small birds, mice.

PLANTS: Indian potatoes (ground nut), various roots and tubers, various seeds, watercress, lupine greens, miner's lettuce, blackberry leaf, mustard greens, mallow weeds, fern shoots, clover, thistle, prickly pear cactus and fruit, mescal leaves and heart, mesquite beans.

MISC: many kinds of mushrooms, grasshoppers, worms, grubs, bugs, honey, ants.

www.ingramcontent.com/pod-product-compliance
Lightning Source LLC
Chambersburg PA
CBHW032048150426
43194CB00006B/456